NON-STOP
CONTAINERS

NON-STOP CONTAINERS

FLOWERING THROUGH THE FOUR SEASONS

Graham Strong

MURDOCH
BOOKS

To my mother, Diana,
from whom I have learnt that gardening
is a pleasure to be shared
and a passion that lasts
a lifetime.

First published 1998 by Merehurst Ltd.
This edition published 2001 by Murdoch Books UK Ltd.

Text copyright © Murdoch Books UK Ltd 1998.
Photography copyright © Graham Strong 1998.

ISBN 1 903002 04 4
A catalogue record for this book is available from the British Library.

Commissioning Editor: **Helen Griffin**
Editor: **Joanna Chisholm**
Designer: **Mason Linklater**

CEO: **Robert Oerton**
Publisher: **Catie Ziller**
Production Manager: **Lucy Byrne**
International Sales Director: **Kevin Lagden**

Murdoch Books UK Ltd
Ferry House, 51–57 Lacy Road,
Putney, London, SW15 1PR, UK
Tel: +44 (0)20 8355 1480
Fax: +44 (0)20 8355 1499
Murdoch Books UK Ltd is a subsidiary
of Murdoch Magazines Pty Ltd.

UK Distribution
Macmillan Distribution Ltd
Houndsmills, Brunell Road
Basingstoke, Hampshire, RG1 6XS, UK
Tel: +44 (0) 1256 302 707
Fax: +44 (0) 1256 351 437
http://www.macmillan-mdl.co.uk

Murdoch Books®
GPO Box 1203
Sydney, NSW 1045, Australia
Tel: +61 (0)2 8220 2000
Fax: +61 (0)2 8220 2020
Murdoch Books® is a trademark
of Murdoch Magazines Pty Ltd.

Contents

Introduction

Containers provide me with some of the most satisfying and exciting high spots in my gardening year and I am convinced that they could do the same for you.

Non-stop Containers is the first book to lay down a photographic record of the life of an individual or group of containers in a real outdoor-garden setting (not a whiter-than-white studio). That's quite a feat, and it has taken four years of planning and planting to complete. This hands-on approach is, I believe, the best way to give an accurate and realistic account of what the aspiring container gardener wants to know: how to maintain a continuous flow of colour and interest from the same range of pots, 365 days a year.

In this book you'll see how terracotta weathers from its raw, freshly fired colour to a mellow patina and learn which clays are frost-proof or prone to flake in winter. You'll find out which plants to raise from seed, how plants increase in size and potential from one year to the next, when to buy mature, specimen-sized plants and use your borders to grow on bedding for pot work, as well as when to return spent plants to the open garden to make permanent, eye-catching groups.

These pages rarely include an isolated individual container such as a single pot on a bare, exposed patio or a hanging basket by a door swinging alone in the breeze. Instead *Non-stop Containers* dovetails neatly into a four-season cycle of planting and growing in which specially prepared locations and settings transform bare paving, tarmac drives, wide paths, beds and borders crying out for a focal point.

CHOOSING YOUR CONTAINERS

Pots, tubs, troughs, urns and baskets are not bought one day and discarded the next like fashion items. You work with what you've got (and of course add to the collection), so rather than present 100 different types I have shown how to succeed at least four times a year with 26 of the most useful and desirable kinds.

The pace never slackens: as well as ever-popular spring and summer displays, increasingly fashionable autumn is given special prominence, and there's no attempt to dodge those winter months when the garden is icebound and nothing seems to stir. My non-stop container recipes have been through heat waves, torrential rain, frost and snow and an occasional missed watering.

Nor do I let enthusiasm gloss over any pitfalls that sooner or later will come your way. Cultivation tips are given throughout the book in the main body of the text, and there are a few additional ones on p.140. A novice however may benefit from the more comprehensive information about basic container-gardening techniques to be found in my book *Pots, Tubs and Containers*, also published by Merehurst.

PERFECT TIMING

In *Non-stop Containers* you'll probably notice that containers are sometimes filled when the plants are in full bloom. If you're unsure about heights and colours, this is a foolproof way to avoid mistakes and with care the plants come to no harm. However planting earlier, when the buds are just visible, will prolong the display period and make it less likely you will damage brittle stems.

Each recipe is accompanied by an indication as to which months it will perform. This will of course vary a little from year to year and more markedly if you garden in an especially cold or warm part of Europe. If not at their peak, all containers can still be occupied all year round.

SOURCING PLANTS

I have included an eclectic blend of annuals, tender and herbaceous perennials, vegetables and herbs, climbers, alpines, shrubs, bulbs and small trees. Common plants rub shoulders with rarer and more sophisticated fare. Some are quite recent introductions, yet all have proved their worth.

Don't worry if you are unable to find the exact variety used. Good substitutes are often given and there are plenty of others that will have a similar height and colour. The same could also be said of the containers themselves. Proportions – height, width and depth – are more important than a specific design.

Nor is it essential to work with an almost limitless variety of plants. Quite often I have included the same plant in different recipes, particularly if they are adaptable, have outstanding qualities or perform over several seasons. With each new outing they take on a different persona.

AWARD OF GARDEN MERIT

Throughout this book I have indicated by the chalice symbol ♀ those plants that have received The Royal Horticultural Society's Award of Garden Merit. This is awarded to a plant of outstanding merit that passes the following criteria: excellent for garden use; good constitution; not particularly susceptible to pests and diseases; does not require specialist care other than the provision of the appropriate growing conditions; and is a distinct and stable form. As you'll see, such plants include some real gems.

CONTINGENCY PLANTS

Container gardening is infectious and, as your horizons expand, you'll begin to find that you can't buy some of the most desirable bulbs and annuals on the point of flower. How often have you seen 'Hollyhock' hyacinths or *Rudbeckia* 'Becky Mixed' for sale as growing plants for example? The answer is to grow your own. Just as the finest borders have a back-up nursery plot from where new blood can be sourced, so the best containers are topped up from a mobile potted nursery where lilies, tulips, autumn *Crocus* and the most desirable, seed-raised strains of *Petunia*, *Phlox* and pansies are waiting in the wings.

A dozen of the most valuable shrubs and herbaceous plants draped around the base of your display container or filling out the back will create a setting that can add considerably to the overall impact. A big *Hosta*, some spreading junipers, *Leucothoe* 'Scarletta' and spurges that are readily accessible can be manna from heaven.

WHEN TO SAY GOODBYE

One of the main attractions of non-stop growing is that you can retain key plants and use them to build a new recipe, thereby saving time and money. However I suspect you would soon tire of a container display that changed very little, apart from the addition of a little seasonal icing – a few primroses here, a couple of *Petunia* there.

Non-stop Containers makes it clear where plants have crossed the divide between seasons, when it's worth persevering with a plant and when it's time to make a fresh start. Leggy pansies, for example, can be disguised among a deep bed of supporting foliage; hellebores may have good foliage, but are not so good that you'd want to keep them in your display pot for a whole year.

PREPARING THE STAGE

At every turn of the page you'll find something different: a novel display idea, a rare plant or a common one looking unexpectedly good, a unique or classic plant combination or a complete theatre especially built to flaunt the recipe container. With this last point in mind, I'm becoming a strong believer that the golden rule for success with containers is the same as for opening a shop: location, location and location. My tulip urn is backed by purple foliage, my ornamental vegetables by sweetcorn and 'Painted Lady' beans, my chrysanths and decorative cabbage are enhanced by Japanese maples, and my primroses by peeling paintwork.

Around the base there are contrasting textures of gravel, pebbles, clay pavers, water-filled bowls, tiny clay pots and patterned paving as well as a variety of floral and foliage plants. Building up the scene like this is great fun and soon you'll have a series of hot spots around the garden to delight yourself and visitors.

In this book I've only just scratched the surface of non-stop container gardening. Although the permutations are endless, just picking out plants at random and planting them in pots is unlikely to succeed. Whether colour-themed creations or cheeky or charming character plants capture your imagination or you're more interested in the exclusive, edible, eye-catching or exotic, you'll find plenty to inspire you here.

DIFFICULTY RATINGS

To help you select a suitable recipe for your garden, I have given each of my 104 recipes a difficulty rating, as follows:

- •   very easy – ideal for novice container gardeners;
- ••   easy – for more experienced gardeners as a little more care and planning are required;
- •••   challenging – for experienced gardeners who are looking for something different; well worth the effort.

The handful of 'challenging' recipes might involve co-ordinating several seed-raised varieties so they peak together or pitting your wits against the elements during the coldest months of the year. Feel free to disagree with my ratings if you wish. For you, *Aster* may grow like mustard and cress.

	SPRING	SUMMER	AUTUMN	WINTER
Oak half barrel	••	•	••	•
Oval terracotta pot	•	••	•	••
Mud bowls and pot	••	••	•	••
Cherub terracotta pots	••	••	••	•
Potato harvesting basket	••	••	•	•••
Salt-glazed bowl and jars	••	••	••	•
Small terracotta pans	•	••	••	•
Large willow basket	••	••	•	••
Terracotta urn	••	•	••	•
Galvanised tin bath	••	••	••	•
Wooden tubs	•	•••	••	•
Decorated terracotta pots	••	••	•••	•
Bamboo trough	••	••	••	•
Victorian watercart	••	••	••	•
Blue-glazed pot	••	•	•	••
Basketwork pot and pans	••	••	•	•
Three-way trough	•	••	••	•
Giant plain terracotta pot	••	•••	••	•
Flat-bottomed wire basket	•	••	•••	••
Wooden hay cart	•	•	••	•
Blue toy chest	••	••	••	••
Antiqued concrete urn	•••	••	••	•
Ceramic pot nest	•••	••	••	•
Shallow baskets	••	••	•••	•
Simulated-stone trough	•	••	•	•
Giant decorated pot	•••	•••	••	••

▷ *While the seasonal display changes, the* Euonymus *hedge remains – a neat concept to set up an alternative, four-season, non-stop container.*

Oak Half Barrel

Half barrels that previously contained whisky, wine or beer are about the best-value containers you can buy and they rarely look out of place in formal or informal settings. Let them weather naturally, or paint the wood and metal hoops in contrasting colours. To increase their lifespan, raise the base up to allow air to circulate.

Height 45cm (18in)
Diameter 65cm (26in)
Weight 25kg (55lb)

Spring

A half barrel is almost a garden in itself, as it allows you to grow sizeable shrubs such as *Camellia* and *Rhododendron*, perennials such as spurge and *Hosta*, popular spring bedding including tulips, wallflowers and double daisies, or a bit of each.

PICK YOUR SPOT

Roll your half barrel into a warm, sheltered spot near a well-trodden path. Such a siting will double the impact of the container, especially against a background of mature shrubs, which will protect it and serve as a foil. Shrubs with coloured leaves are particularly useful here. To give the barrel an air of permanence, add plants such as these wild strawberries and forget-me-nots around the base.

Pot-grown tulips were used to achieve this wonderful uniformity, and you can lift your forget-me-nots from a border. Start planting from the back of the barrel and move forwards so you have plenty of elbow room. Finish off with the edging.

Pull out the tulips as soon as the petals fall and heel them into the ground to die down. Store the dry bulbs in a shed for planting out in autumn.

BULB NURSERY

Generally, if you plant a dozen bulbs, for one reason or another only nine or ten will develop uniformly. However, if you grow your bulbs in small plastic pots and transfer them to the display container when in bud, you can be sure that every one blooms in precisely the right spot.

EDGE WITH A HEDGE

A necklace of *Euonymus fortunei* 'Emerald 'n' Gold'♥ makes a fine, permanent, evergreen hedge for a barrel and, if it is viewed from the front, you need to plant only about two-thirds of the circumference (about five plants). *Euonymus* gives a soft, informal edge (or a formal one if you clip it) that acts as a frame for your theatre in the round.

I thought I'd been a bit daring with this line-up. Firstly, the colour scheme was bright yellow, which generates its own light – even on dull days. Secondly, if you site the barrel where the taller plants will be backlit by the sun for at least part of the day, it could end up looking as dramatic as this.

On a practical note, I used 'West Point' tulips (the best lily-flowered yellow) above 'Cloth of Gold' wallflowers (*Erysimum*), a meadow of sumptuous Persian buttercups (*Ranunculus asiaticus* 'Accolade') with all-yellow pansies peeping out at intervals. Grow your wallflowers from seed and plant them with the tulips in autumn; then fill in with buttercups and pansies in April. Afterwards sit back and bask in the golden glow.

▷ *Inspired by the egg-yolk centres of the 'Purissima' tulips, I added 'Golden Melody' tulips and double buttercups as well as an edging of yellow feverfew interplanted with forget-me-nots.*

Summer

To gardeners familiar with half barrels, the summer months are a time of heightened expectancy because such a sizeable container can bring fruition to your wildest garden fantasies. I'd often flirted with the idea of growing a scented spire of sweet peas in a tub, but when the results outshone those in the border, I couldn't resist adding more of my favourite, aromatic plants and a seat, to turn the area into a scented retreat.

COMPLETE COVERAGE

Select a dwarf, medium or tall-growing strain of sweet pea to suit the height of your wigwam. I sowed my sweet peas in autumn, three to a 9cm (3½in) pot, and overwintered them in a cold frame. Such autumn-sown seeds will produce earlier, larger and more robust sweet peas than those sown in late winter or early spring, as long as you deter mice. Alternatively you can buy pot-grown plants in spring. Plant the sweet peas in the half barrel in April, removing the tips to encourage them to bush out.

MIND THE GAP

If the base of the planting begins to look a bit thin by July and August why not plug the gaps with a selection of pot-grown, scented-leaved plants pushed in between the uprights. You won't be able to resist running your fingers through the leaves to release the fruity smells of lemon verbena and pineapple sage or the more pungent and spicy curry plant. A pot-pourri of petals and leaves will prolong the memory through dark, winter days.

MORE IDEAS FOR SUMMER

This book includes many stopping-off points, where you may decide to call a halt and enjoy what you've got until the very last flower has faded. However, if like me you are always eager to

△ *Half way up the sweet pea wigwam I tied in the wire hanging basket as a platform on which I sat a pot of trailing, pink* Nemesia denticulata *'Confetti'.*

press on with the next planting combination, here is a scheme to carry your barrel through from late spring (or early summer) to late summer, or even autumn if you wish. It may also make regular replanting of your barrel even more appealing.

RISING STARS

There's no doubt that fashion-conscious gardeners are at present finding ornamental onions such as *Allium cristophii* ♀ highly digestible and if you put them alongside a blue-blooded *Hosta* such as 'Krossa Regal' ♀ and a top-of-the-range *Dicentra* such as this 'Stuart Boothman' ♀ you can't help but impress the most discerning plant connoisseur. However such a planting scheme can also be practical: some pansies get tall and lanky by late June, and a nest of foliage disguises their bare stems. If you're careful you can even dig them up from a border.

The best way to grow the ornamental onions is to plant them individually in 13cm (5in) pots in autumn and pop them into the barrel when the buds begin to show. Their leaves unfortunately are a big letdown – limp and frazzled – and are best submerged by the 'Krossa Regal' *Hosta*, which has unique poise and very long flower spikes.

◁ *Tall, leggy pansies and unsightly ornamental onion foliage can be neatly hidden away among* Hosta *leaves and that permanent* Euonymus *hedge seen on page 10.*

▷ *Pull up a chair, sit back in the sun and soak up the wonderful aromas and colours of your perfumed retreat.*

▷ *Create a spectacular bank of colour around your barrel and you'll extend summer's intensity of bloom well into the autumn.*

Autumn

Autumnal flowers are as good as many colourful leaves. Choose non-trailing nasturtiums for the centre of the barrel – types such as Whirlybird Series with its upward-facing flowers. Sown in late April in pots, they were captured here in late September and continued to the first serious frost. To keep pace with them, rock daisies and *Scaevola* drip an unceasing torrent of blue flowers.

I was enjoying myself so much that I decided to introduce more plants on the ground to give a seamless bank of colour. The barrel was almost completely hidden (you can see the rim by the Chinese lanterns).

After flowering, plant the chrysanth and possibly the Chinese lantern in a border, but be warned: Chinese lantern is very vigorous and will fill your garden faster even than mint.

△ *In autumn, Chinese lanterns lose their skins leaving the fruits swinging in a fragile cage.*

Winter

Winter may be the lowest point in the gardening year, but you can still make your garden work a bit harder and lay on an ice-breaking display in your half barrel. My arrangement here uses readily available plants and materials.

WARMING TO THE THEME

To radiate a little winter warmth, make a living fire with yellow foliage plants for the flames and red buds, leaves and berries for the glowing embers. Pack them in tightly and they will protect each other from penetrating frosts. Look for contrasting shapes for a lively display: cone-shaped with rounded, trailing and cascading. The barrel has not moved since it was shown on the opposite page, but now the evergreens beyond offer shelter and highlights.

△ 'Tête-à-Tête' daffodils never looked better than when peeping out of my red glow of Skimmia japonica 'Rubella' flowers and the foliage of Leucothoe 'Scarletta' in March.

△ To complement the fireplace theme above I nailed some kindling (apple tree prunings) to the barrel front in a primitive, criss-cross, Celtic pattern.

◁ The winter barrel was positioned in a sunny, sheltered spot on a handsome, circular plinth, made with granite setts, bricks and pebbles. Avoid an easterly aspect, where frosted buds and blooms may be damaged by early sunshine.

WINTER RECIPE

JAN	FEB	MAR	APR	MAY	JUN
JUL	AUG	SEP	OCT	NOV	DEC

YOU WILL NEED

- 1 mature, yellow, dwarf Lawson cypress (*Chamaecyparis lawsoniana* 'Minima Aurea' ♚) (1)
- 1 sawara cypress (*C. pisifera* 'Filifera Aurea' ♚) (2)
- 1 *Leucothoe* 'Scarletta' (3)
- 1 small-leaved, variegated ivy (*Hedera helix* 'Chicago') (4)
- 2 *Gaultheria procumbens* ♚ (5)
- 1 *Skimmia japonica* 'Rubella' ♚ (6)
- broken polystyrene chunks or crocks
- 120 litres ericaceous (lime-free) potting compost

GOOD SUBSTITUTES

Plant *Thuja orientalis* 'Aurea Nana' ♚ or *T. occidentalis* 'Rheingold' ♚ as the background conifer.

FOR CONTINUITY

Tuck in some pot-grown daffodils like these ever-popular 'Tête-à-Tête' ♚, which are widely available from February onwards. 'Jumblie' daffodils are similar to 'Tête-à-Tête'.

ALTERNATIVELY

For other ways to use *Skimmia japonica* 'Rubella' see page 108.

Oval Terracotta Pot

It's well worth investing in top-quality, hand-made terracotta pots. This oval pot is a delight with its pressed garland decorations, and shaped somewhere between a pot and a trough.

Height 23cm (9in)
Width 23cm (9in)
Length 43cm (17in)
Weight 11kg (24lb)

Spring

The importance of matching the scale of your plants to their container is easily overlooked. A 'King Alfred'-sized daffodil would be a disaster in this spring pot, and in each of the five planting ideas seen here and over the page I have not overpowered my oval pot.

Miniature forms of daffodils are riding the crest of a wave now, which is not surprising since each bulb produces several flower spikes of sometimes-scented blooms at a time when larger trumpet types may be going over. These 'Minnow' daffodils were really prolific producing all these stems from just 15 bulbs. Their primrose centre is picked up by the pansies below. Plant them both in autumn.

△ *Keep the spring planting scheme simple and use colour to link your collection.*

Summer

A traditionally made pot does not have be filled with old-fashioned plants. This summer selection of new cultivars also suits older-style containers such as my oval pot and is testament to the skills of modern plant breeders and nurserymen.

SMALLER ROOTBALLS
To plug a small gap at the front of a container that is too narrow for a typical bedding plant rootball, grow plants in plastic cell trays that give the roots and compost a bullet-shaped profile. I tracked down this red form of *Alternanthera* for my summer pot. Along with *Viola*, it makes a lively edge that lasts all summer. Sow your sunflowers in individual 9cm (3½in) pots and transfer them to the display pot when green flower buds show.

◁ *Alternanthera, a plant generally more familiar in floral clocks, here makes an exotic mini-hedge to contain these* Viola *and sunflowers.*

▷ *Ultra dwarf sunflowers such as 'Big Smile' take fewer than 100 days from seed to flower. These were sown in April and are shown here in late July.*

LATE SUMMER STUNNERS

They may seem an unlikely pairing, but dwarf *Aster* and coleus are made for each other. The *Aster* can be bought in May and June as bedding plants or even in bud and flower from mid-summer onwards. When grown from seed, wilt can be a problem even on quite mature plants. I have found that by delaying indoor sowing until April when there is less chance of cold, damp weather, plants are less prone to this disease. I grew these *Aster* 'Carpet Ball Mixed' from seed.

Coleus such as these 'Dragon Sunset and Volcano Mixed' can be raised from seed too, but need to be sown earlier – in February or early March in a heated propagator. Named varieties grown from cuttings often have more spectacular leaf shapes and colour. Coleus needs a warm, sheltered spot to do well outdoors and a sunny window indoors. Remember to keep pinching out the flowers to retain the leaf quality.

◁ *Aster and coleus make a fine, late-summer partnership as they weave through each other like this.*

AUTUMN RECIPE

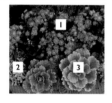

JAN	FEB	MAR	APR	MAY	JUN
JUL	AUG	SEP	OCT	NOV	DEC

YOU WILL NEED

- 4 or 5 dwarf michaelmas daisies (*Aster novi-belgii*) (1)
- 2 pots variegated *Euonymus japonicus* 'Microphyllus Aureovariegatus' or similar (2)
- 2 pink, medium-sized ornamental cabbage (3)
- broken polystyrene chunks or crocks
- 14 litres multipurpose potting compost

GOOD SUBSTITUTES

Look for the smallest forms of chrysanth such as *Chrysanthemum* 'Robin' as a back row.

Autumn

For some autumn container recipes you need plenty of advance planning, sowing seed, planting bulbs and preening the cast for its garden premiere. Others require much less dedication but cost more. This is one of the latter. You can buy your plants, bring them home and within ten minutes you have an instant showpiece.

Working from back to front to prevent compost spills on your front rows, plant the michaelmas daisies across the back of the oval pot. Next, tease apart the rooted cuttings within the rootball of your potted *Euonymus*, unrolling these to fit around opposite sides of the rim. Then add the two pink cabbages. Sink the rootballs into the pot so the rosette of leaves is just above the rim. Angle them forward so they beam out at you. Top up with more potting compost and spray off any spills. Place the pot near a colouring maple or *Berberis*, and you'll have the very essence of autumn.

▷ *Angle the ornamental cabbages forward a little so they lean out from among the daisies.*

Winter

A well-drained, home-produced terracotta pot like this can be left outdoors all year round, so why not fill it with contrasting evergreens?

Before you start, consider the angle from which you'll be viewing the pot. Dwarf bulbs for example should be in front of taller evergreens if it's against a wall. For a change I decided to position my oval pot so that it was seen from the side. This meant I'd be looking at a banked-up wall of colour rather than thin lines.

In winter, when gardens are stripped back to their bare essentials, you can really appreciate the elements, such as texture, shape and colour, that combine to give a satisfying plant grouping. The fine, spiky texture of the *Cryptomeria* and winter heather here contrast with the medium-textured, variegated *Euonymus* and the coarse-textured *Tellima* at the front. In this terracotta pot all plants have a similar, rounded habit so there's no contrast there, yet the yellowy green of the *Euonymus* attractively offsets the red-brown and bronze foliage and is the perfect backdrop for the earliest cultivars of *Iris reticulata* ♀.

◁ *Look out for these chemically dwarfed michaelmas daisies in garden centres from late summer.*

◁ *An overwintered pot can be crammed with plenty of plants as they will make no appreciable growth.*

As the weather gets colder, the food store in winter-colouring plants turns from starch to oil and the resulting leaf colours are surprisingly variable: deep reds, chocolate-brown, bronze and even a touch of pink. Then as temperatures rise in spring, they change back to green (or bronzy green). Such plants are excellent when mixed with yellow and grey foliage so in your winter creations why not include *Chamaecyparis thyoides* 'Ericoides' ♀, *Leucothoe walteri* 'Rainbow', *Microbiota decussata* ♀ and *Erica carnea* 'Vivellii' ♀ as well as the two shown here.

A winter heather is almost compulsory and 'Kramer's Rote' is early to bloom with extra-long flower spikes. *Iris* you can buy as dry bulbs in October. Pot them up three to a 9cm (3½in) pot, and tuck them in around the heather in February. Alternatively you can plant the bulbs directly in the display pot in autumn, or buy them in flower in early spring.

◁ *Mix colourful evergreens with winter heathers and bulbs for a pot brimming with variety and interest.*

WINTER RECIPE

JAN	FEB	MAR	APR	MAY	JUN
JUL	AUG	SEP	OCT	NOV	DEC

YOU WILL NEED

- 1 dwarf *Cryptomeria japonica* 'Elegans Compacta' ♀ (1)
- 1 mature winter heather (*Erica* x *darleyensis* 'Kramer's Rote' ♀, syn. 'Kramer's Red') (2)
- 1 *Euonymus fortunei* 'Emerald 'n' Gold' ♀ (3)
- 1 *Tellima grandiflora* Rubra Group 'Purpurea' (4)
- 10 dwarf *Iris* 'Harmony' (5)
- broken polystyrene chunks or crocks
- 14 litres potting compost

GOOD SUBSTITUTES

Iris reticulata 'J. S Dijt' is purple, 'Cantab' is Cambridge blue and the earliest of all *Iris danfordiae* is yellow.

FOR CONTINUITY

Plant the *Iris* in a sunny, well-drained bed, although you'll be lucky if they increase. Even if they don't, their violet perfume will convince you they are worth it. Replace them with pot-grown *Anemone blanda* ♀.

Mud Bowls and Pot

These dark brown, Thai mud bowls and pot have a raw, earthy quality that blends well with informal planting schemes. They are also impervious to frost. To form a cluster of contrasting heights and diameters, you'll need at least three of them.

POT	SMALL BOWL	LARGE BOWL
Height	Height	Height
30cm (12in)	15cm (6in)	23cm (9in)
Diameter	Diameter	Diameter
33cm (13in)	23cm (9in)	40cm (16in)
Weight	Weight	Weight
10kg (22lb)	2kg (4½lb)	9kg (20lb)

Spring

If you want to set yourself a challenge, why not pick out some 'difficult' colours from the autumn bulb catalogues. It's hard enough to describe the colour of 'Gipsy Queen' hyacinths let alone choose a partner for them, but these peachy pink polyanthus worked well. The large, buff-patterned bowl also proved to be the perfect match for my scheme. Yellow, orange-nosed daffodils made an excellent backdrop.

SHADES OF PEACH

You may have to search around for the polyanthus. Mine were lifted from a border, split and replanted when they had finished flowering. One of the cheaper seed mixtures (without the giant flowers) will give you the best selection. Plant both bulbs and bedding in autumn.

△ *Adventurous mixtures of hyacinths and polyanthus can give truly stunning colour schemes in spring.*

Summer

As an antidote to those house facades where every brick is concealed behind hyperactive *Petunia* and busy lizzies, why not create a calming oasis of leaves and cool blue and white flowers. You can almost sense a fall in temperature as you wander into its embrace.

LUSCIOUS LEAVES

Foliage pots of herbaceous perennials will give months of interest, although their leaves are at their best in the first half of summer. Alternatively you could select flowering plants that also have good foliage.

All the varieties in my summer creation can be bought at the sizes shown on the right, so this recipe will appeal to even the most impatient gardener. Solomon's seal makes an elegant upper storey in the large bowl above bugle, meadowsweet, *Hosta* and sweet woodruff.

FEAST OF FLOWERS

▷ *A pile of sticks on a woodland fringe makes the perfect backdrop for this summer collection of foliage plants.*

Here's an eye-popping display of flower colour that doesn't degenerate into a nasty riot and, providing you restrict the colour range, you don't need to include the rare or exclusive to make your mark. For the latter half of summer, *Fuchsia* 'Lady Thumb'♀ and floss flower (*Ageratum*) will lend soft, pastel colours while dwarf *Aster* such as 'Milady Mixed' try to steal the show.

Extend the theme to two other pots or bowls featuring pale blue, trailing *Lobelia* and pink *Diascia*, purple heliotrope (*Heliotropium arborescens* 'Chatsworth'♀) for scent, *Helichrysum petiolare* 'Goring Silver' for foliage and perhaps pale pink Junior *Petunia* for flower power.

◁ Fuchsia *and* Aster *are naturally late developers, unlike floss flowers, which you'll need to sow in April – a little later than usual – to ensure they are in their prime at the same time as the other flowers.*

Autumn

Large-flowered spring *Crocus* clustered in grass around whitewashed silver birch trees never fails to please, but have you ever thought of repeating the idea in autumn with autumn crocus and ornamental grasses in a shallow bowl? It looks great and couldn't be simpler to arrange.

ORNAMENTAL GRASSES

At your local garden centre, select five of your favourite ornamental grasses, aiming for a range of habits, heights and leaf colours. The sedge *Carex hachijoensis* 'Evergold'♀ is tailor-made to curl over the rim of the large mud bowl, while variegated purple moor grass makes a net curtain of flower spikes behind.

Then pick out six plump autumn crocus bulbs that have begun to sprout on the shop shelves. Work them in among the grasses, then sit back and wait for the bulbs to flower.

△ A vibrant mix of Colchicum *and grasses is very much at the leading edge of gardening fashion.*

Winter

If you have a suitably warm and sheltered position in your garden, I would recommend one of the most refined hellebores of them all. Its leaves are blue green with paler veins and midribs, the stems, leaf petioles and flower buds are flushed with red, and its cupped flowers each produce a great boss of yellow stamens. I bought it as a *Helleborus lividus*♀ hybrid, but it is obviously very close to the slightly tender *H. lividus*, which is native to Majorca. It has survived two years outdoors with hardly any sign of the leaf-spot disease that afflicts other members of the hellebore family. But how can you make the most of this prized discovery?

PLANT IN LAYERS

For a really full, action-packed display, plant up the large mud bowl in tiers. The upper canopy is provided by the hellebore with winter heather and yellow *Euonymus* piercing through its leaves. Below them, the rim is softened by a mother-of-thousands – a plant that is more familiar as a houseplant to many people.

FORGE A LINK

If you include enough of one colour or plant in an individual container, it will soon start to blend together and work as a set. Plant the small mud bowl with a single species such as ruddy-leaved *Leucothoe* in the foreground. Position the bowl so it overlaps the deep purple heathers in the large bowl behind. The mud pot also contains more of the same heather variety, as well as red pernettya berries. To lighten it up, I included some brightly coloured evergreens to contrast with all those reds and purples.

The containers were raised up on sections of logs set in gravel. They looked like islands rising out of a shifting sea. Why not make a similar base for your pots. Mine greeted me with a warm glow on those cold, wet, winter days, and made a real splash.

△ *The hellebore creates an almost tree-like canopy, adding height and character to the bowl.*

▷ *Position the three bowls in a triangle with the tallest bowl at the back and let the plants flow through each other.*

▷▷ *Don't let the seed from your hellebore go to waste. In June harvest the ripe pods before they spill their seed. Sow seed at once in a seed tray and overwinter the tray in a cold frame. A year later you will have plants like these to grow on and swap with friends.*

WINTER RECIPE

JAN	FEB	MAR	APR	MAY	JUN
JUL	AUG	SEP	OCT	NOV	DEC

YOU WILL NEED

- 1 hellebore (*Helleborus lividus* hybrid) (1)
- 3 mature winter heathers (*Erica* × *darleyensis* 'Kramer's Rote'♀, syn. 'Kramer's Red') (2)
- 1 *Euonymus* 'Blondy' (3)
- 1 mother-of-thousands (*Saxifraga stolonifera*♀) (4)
- 1 ruddy-leaved *Leucothoe* 'Scarletta' (5)
- 1 *Erica* × *darleyensis* 'Arthur Johnson'♀ (6)
- 1 red-berried, female pernettya (*Gaultheria mucronata*♀) (7)
- 1 *Leucothoe walteri* 'Rainbow' (8)
- 5 *Crocus tommasinianus*♀ (9)
- broken polystyrene chunks or crocks
- 45 litres ericaceous (lime-free) potting compost

GOOD SUBSTITUTES

Helleborus × *sternii* is similar to *H. lividus* and hardier.

FOR CONTINUITY

Slip in pots of dwarf bulbs as they come into season. When the winter heathers are over, trim off the old flowers and plant them in a bed with the bulbs in between. For another crop of berries always plant a female pernettya near to a male one.

JAN	FEB	MAR	APR	MAY	JUN
JUL	AUG	SEP	OCT	NOV	DEC

YOU WILL NEED

♦ 20 'Prinses Irene' tulips ♀ (1)
♦ 9–12 orange and yellow Siberian wallflowers (*Erysimum* × *allionii* ♀) (2)
♦ 5 dwarf, blue forget-me-nots (*Myosotis*) (3)
♦ broken polystyrene chunks or crocks
♦ 36 litres multipurpose potting compost for the large pot and 10 litres for the small pot

GOOD SUBSTITUTES

Golden-orange 'Generaal de Wet' tulips, with their delicious fragrance, are equally noteworthy.

▽ *Ever keen for more colour, I hid some pots of 'Union Jack' tulips between the terracotta to rise up through the Choisya foliage.*

Cherub Terracotta Pots

These charming Italian terracotta pots with winged cherubs have straight sides, which allow them to hold more potting compost than sloping-sided ones. They're competitively priced but only guaranteed frost-resistant not frost-proof, so they should be wrapped up or taken indoors during frosty spells.

Spring

Finding a theme for a springtime spectacular is easier if you let your tulip selection dictate the company it keeps (pansies can be similarly influential, as we shall see later). The much-heralded 'Prinses Irene' tulip deserves every accolade in all departments: it has waxy, blue-green leaves and petals licked by darker, flame-shaped markings on the outside.

Plant your tulip bulbs in October or November, three or four to a 13cm (5in) pot, then transfer them to the large cherub pot in April along with your pot-grown wallflowers. Add dwarf forget-me-nots lifted from a border and more plants of a sunny disposition, such as *Origanum vulgare* 'Aureum' ♀ and *Choisya ternata* 'Sundance' ♀, around the base.

AUGUST SOWING

Siberian wallflowers are hardier, later into bloom and more free-flowering than the more familiar gillies. You'll rarely find them in garden centres in late summer, so you'll need to sow your own.

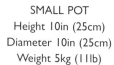

SMALL POT	LARGE POT
Height 10in (25cm)	Height 16in (40cm)
Diameter 10in (25cm)	Diameter 15in (38cm)
Weight 5kg (11lb)	Weight 28kg (62lb)

△ *Solomon's seal, Welsh poppies and forget-me-nots can be dug up from borders to make an alternative spring recipe.*

WEATHERING POTS

New terracotta often has a rather harsh, red tone to it, but will weather quickly if you paint on live yoghurt. A black pin mould appears first, followed by algal growth on the ledges where the clay stays damp and then lime deposits that leach naturally from the clay. The large empty cherub pot seen at the top of this page was given this yoghurt treatment six months before it was photographed. To soften its appearance, I brushed the smaller cherub pot with a thin solution of lime and water.

▷ *You couldn't wish for a more harmonious pairing than 'Prinses Irene' tulips and orange and yellow Siberian wallflowers.*

Summer

Any plant such as Siberian wallflowers that flowers from spring to summer has to be doubly welcome because it fills the gap until annuals and bedding plants get into their stride.

YEAR-ROUND INTEREST

To maintain a container at fever pitch, top it up with new plants as others go over; I managed to keep my cherub pots brimming with colour from tulip time to the autumn frosts.

In late May, I collected up the fallen tulip petals and put them in the dustbin (they can spread tulip fire disease). I then lifted them and heeled them in on some spare ground. When they'd died down, I dried them off for autumn planting. You may prefer to plant them into a sunny border straight away. Meanwhile I added two double handfuls of fresh potting compost to the large pot and planted up some 'Jolly Joker' pansies. After another three weeks I dug up the wallflowers and forget-me-nots.

COLOURFUL KALE

For phase three I introduced 'Red Chidori' ornamental kale, which gives good colour in summer and exceptional tints in autumn. You may come across some for sale in early July but, to be sure, raise your own plants from seed. If you want monster rosettes that will be better able to withstand the cold and look more impressive too, sow ornamental cabbages and kale early. These were sown indoors on 3 March.

Yellow is a delight with rich purple so I bought two slipper flowers and tried some seed-raised 'Golden Emperor' nasturtiums alongside. Again replenishing the compost, I packed them into the large cherub pot and within a week they had woven together to form a vividly colourful tapestry. For the foreground, I placed a potful of *Nemesia* 'KLM' just where the pansies could trail down into its blossom.

△ *Yellow and orange flowers look particularly good rising up among the rich purple rosettes of ornamental kale. The pansy wing petals also provide a colour link.*

◁ *Irrepressible 'Jolly Joker' pansies are the perfect replacement for the tulips and keep flowering for the rest of the summer.*

◁ *Whatever the weather you can always rely on 'Red Chidori' kale to greet you with a beaming smile!*

▷ *Seek out those green seed pods hiding among the pansy and nasturtium leaves.*

DEADHEADING

Some summer bedders will flower until the frosts as long as you water them; others such as pansies require a little more care. Pansies need regular deadheading; don't wait until the green, beak-like pods appear. Nip off the flowerhead as soon as the petals start to curl. Nasturtiums too can look unkempt unless you pick off yellowing leaves and limp flowers.

In late August the large cherub pot still looked marvellous, helped by a double helping of French marigolds alongside, as you'll see top right.

JUST LILIES

With such a wide array of container plants to tempt us, it's easy to end up using too many types. Sometimes the simplest ideas give the greatest satisfaction. Lilies for example excel in pots – even the taller varieties – and to set them off all they need is groundcover at the roots to cast a little shade and add a complementary colour.

Cherub pots are ideal for lilies, having the depth that encourages rooting up the stem and the weight that keeps them stable in windy weather. I planted six 'Royal Queen' lily bulbs half way down the large pot in a triangle in March. I then interplanted three catmints (*Nepeta* 'Six Hills Giant').

After flowering, I planted out the arrangement in a border for a scaled-up, repeat performance the following year.

▷ *Position your lily pot near a main door and you'll be greeted by a wall of intoxicating perfume in July and August.*

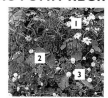

Autumn

Although it's a waste to fill a decorated pot with vigorous trailers, I decided a half-concealed cherub might be intriguing. In fact planting *Zinnia*, double nasturtium and double chamomile together was an experiment. In terms of staying power, these three can last well into autumn despite the odd weekend without water. The double flowers last for weeks since, unable to set seed, the petals don't fall. Incidentally the blue borage and heart-shaped leaves of *Asarina* – also in my cherub pot – were self-sown.

DOUBLE FLOWERS

I'm surprised double-flowering chamomile is not seen far more often in pots mixed in with other herbs and scented pelargoniums. It sprouts early in the year and the leaves have a gorgeous smell. Double nasturtiums are now freely available, thanks to modern, intensive propagation techniques. They really are a treasure and far easier to grow than the much-publicised double *Lobelia*. Root cuttings of the nasturtiums and give them away as an insurance in case yours die. They need a heated greenhouse to overwinter.

△ *If you've tried and failed with other* Zinnia *grow* 'Starbright Mixed', *but don't sow it too early: May will do. In autumn it flowers well even in dull spells.*

Winter

For sophistication, hardiness and length of flowering, the Lenten rose has to be the supreme winter performer. Even in April, the slate-grey and purple varieties are still colourful. Most of mine were grown from seed so there is considerable variation in flower colour and the degree to which each bloom nods over, though almost all are worth keeping.

EYE LEVEL

We used weeping willow wands and short prunings to tie up the flower stems as well as raising the pot on feet so the blooms were nearer to eye level. Around the edge of the pot we planted some lusty polyanthus to scent the air with their evocative perfume. If they're still presentable, you don't have to cut away the old Lenten rose leaves, though it can make a plant more manageable.

△ *Pull the Lenten rose stalks back a little so that you can greet the blooms face to face during winter.*

▷ *Buy Lenten roses in flower so you can see exactly what's coming. The range is mouth-watering, as you'll see from these cut blooms, which are part of the 'Ashwood Hybrid' range.*

These utilitarian, galvanised wire baskets have quickly become one of the most sought-after garden accessories to have slung under your arm or, better still, planted with a lavish show of foliage and flowers. Stronger than wicker, they can be suspended from a tree or bracket and hold enough compost to satisfy a wide range of planting styles.

Height 18cm (7in)
Width 33cm (13in)
Length 45cm (18in)
Weight 2kg (4½lb)

Spring

Once you've tried all the most popular spring bedding, you begin to thirst for more unusual plants or imaginative ways to use common ones. My spring harvesting basket satisfies both desires and is held together by a vein of purple leaves that adds richness to the flowers.

The spurge and bugle are forms of British native plants, the wild form of the exotic buttercup comes from Asia and the remarkable blue *Corydalis* is from China. They'd look good together in any sort of hanging basket.

▷ *It may require a little more effort and expense but this dangling spring collection makes a welcome change from tulips and pansies.*

Summer

Nothing is more satisfying than growing something you can eat. I set out to make my basket both decorative and productive by using whitefly-deterring French marigolds alongside the tomatoes, growing edible flowers such as nasturtiums (you can also eat the leaves and seed pods) and including curly-leaved parsley, basil and a decorative kale to garnish the salad.

DECORATIVE AND FRUITFUL

Although my edible basket could have been suspended, I thought it looked better alongside a path near the kitchen door, basking against a backdrop of herbs. Choose a dwarf, bush or trailing tomato or you'll have two feet of stem before the first truss appears. Sow the nasturtiums and marigolds indoors in April and the basil, which hates to be checked by a cold spell, in early May unless you have a heated greenhouse.

△ *For a change of mood, go for a leafy line-up in summer by sowing a mixture of salad leaves alongside parsley, with borage, nasturtiums and pot marigolds providing the edible flowers.*

▷ *Position your summer basket by a border of herbs and rest it on a flowerpot to deter slugs and you'll have a feast for the eye and the taste buds.*

COLLECTOR'S PIECE

Some plants, especially new ones, can be extremely difficult to buy but after much searching I did eventually track down *Silene dioica* 'Thelma Kay' and it was worth the wait. Its yellow-veined leaves and pink, powder-puff flowers blend beautifully. I slipped it in behind the bugle from the spring basket, which was now romping over the edge, and let the *Silene*'s pink flowers spill over too.

Building on the yellow-variegated theme, I added variegated London pride (*Saxifraga × urbium* 'Variegata') and variegated meadow foxtail grass (*Alopecurus pratensis* 'Aureovariegatus'). The basket looked a gem and those blue spikes of bugle flowers were never better. You may need to spray the leaves against mildew however, preferably before the powdery white, tell-tale signs appear.

◁ *Both the foliage and flowers of 'Thelma Kay' and bugle contrasted beautifully together. All they needed was grass-like and rosette-shaped leaves to complete the composition.*

△ *Cast your container adrift in a sea of forget-me-nots. Sink a pot a few centimetres into the ground to make a pedestal then hide it with your basket.*

AUTUMN RECIPE

JAN	FEB	MAR	APR	MAY	JUN
JUL	AUG	SEP	OCT	NOV	DEC

YOU WILL NEED

- ‣ 'Arran Victory' potatoes (1)
- ‣ 'Tigerella'♀ and 'Gardener's Delight'♀ tomatoes (2)
- ‣ 'Red Baron' onions (3)
- ‣ a mixture of cut herbs (4)
- ‣ hay for lining the basket
- ‣ 2 small willow baskets and a water reservoir

Autumn

The traditional gathering-in of the harvest and the celebration of summer's bounty are instilled in us from early childhood, and there are few gardeners who do not get a real thrill from laying out their produce. With this basket display you can make a handsome showcase for your harvest in the kitchen or porch. It would also make an ideal gift for an enthusiastic cook.

HARVEST FESTIVAL

Line the basket with hay, then twist some strands together to make a thick length of 'rope' to trim the edge. Set two small willow baskets inside, one with a jar or bucket for the cut herbs. Then gather your ingredients. There are some remarkable shapes and colours to tickle your fancy.

Start with potatoes, then work in tomatoes, red onions and finally a selection of the most useful culinary herbs, such as basil, apple mint, parsley and marjoram, bunched together in the water-filled reservoir. What a treat: healthy eating in technicolor tints.

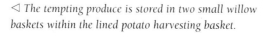

◁ *The tempting produce is stored in two small willow baskets within the lined potato harvesting basket.*

△ *Some fruits and vegetables are so attractive it's a shame to eat them. Potatoes come in all shapes and sizes – and amazing colours too.*

Winter

If a potato harvesting basket pierced with conifer trimmings looks like a nest, then crocus tulips poking their red, beak-like blooms out of the centre are the baby birds peering out for a meal. The only problem is that a great deal of winter sunlight is needed to tease open the tulip petals and reveal their dark inner markings. However there is nothing else like them this early in the year.

BULB NEST

Use conifer trimmings such as these from a Leyland cypress to line the potato harvesting basket. I then covered the trimmings with black plastic sheeting before adding the compost. Next I jabbed in more conifer sprigs, angling them so they arched downwards. Finally I was ready to plant the bulbs.

△ *This trio of bulbs may present a challenge but I can guarantee it will be the most refined spring basket around your neighbourhood.*

FORWARD PLANNING

To achieve this level of uniformity at flowering time, pot up the tulips and *Crocus* into 10cm (4in) pots in autumn. Order 'in the green' snowdrops in spring from a specialist supplier and pot them the year before they are required or buy pot-grown ones when you are ready to plant up your winter basket. Alternatively dig up your own when the leaves begin to show. Don't use dry bulbs, because they will not give quick enough results.

Transfer the snowdrops and *Crocus* to the basket in February. Line the *Crocus* along the basket edge so they spill over into the conifer sprigs. Add the tulips and suspend the basket from a bracket or branch in a warm, sheltered spot. In poor weather, move the basket into a porch, conservatory or greenhouse.

◁ *Sunlight is essential to bring out the beauty within these eye-catching blooms.*

▷ *Once you've positioned these bulb-filled, salt-glazed containers, add foliage plants and spurges on the margins to build up the picture.*

Salt-glazed Bowl and Jars

Salt-glazed containers have a characteristic shine and subtle variation in colour achieved by throwing salt into the kiln during firing. Being impervious to moisture, they are far less likely to flake during frosty weather than the more popular, imported, terracotta ones. Unlike terracotta, they don't weather appreciably except for a little algal growth.

Spring

Bulbs and fireworks have a great deal in common. Both are surprise packages ready to burst forth into a galaxy of stars. You couldn't dream up a more convenient way to garden, and most gardeners succumb to their allure.

Keukenhof – the Dutch showcase for some of the nine billion bulbs they grow each year – is undeniably spectacular but, without shrubs and herbaceous plants alongside, is a little overpowering. My bulb showcase is far more modest, and sets out to combine a range of complementary plants that help to reveal the unique qualities of each bulb.

DOUBLE STANDARDS
You either love double daffodils or you hate them! The more full doubles are top heavy and can topple over in wet weather, but that's when you cut them for the vase – where they last very well. I used some gnarled pieces of wood to prop up my 'Tahiti'. For a really full pot, plant ten bulbs in a double layer. I elevated their pot on a upturned flowerpot to fill out the rear stalls in my bulb theatre, where they picked up the orange-red of the crown imperials in the bowl below.

IMPERIAL HIGHNESS
Crown imperials are beguiling plants and their flowers peer down in a rather superior manner. It's rewarding to enjoy them in a container for the first year before planting them out permanently. I underplanted them with grape hyacinths, though in hindsight a blue hyacinth would have had more impact. Wallflowers add cottage-garden charm here alongside the invaluable sawara cypress.

It's useful to have specimen foliage plants such as purple-leaved *Berberis* and yellow-variegated *Euonymus* as a foil behind regularly staged groups of containers. *Euphorbia characias* subsp. *wulfenii*♀ (behind the crown imperials) is also a classic foil in leaf and flower.

BOWL	SMALL JAR	TALL JAR
Height	Height	Height
28cm (11in)	30cm (12in)	63cm (25in)
Diameter	Diameter	Diameter
38cm (15in)	20cm (8in)	25cm (10in)
Weight	Weight	Weight
10kg (22lb)	5kg (11lb)	25kg (55lb)

▷ *These delightful spring bulbs deserve a special setting of their own. They'll look far better than single varieties grown in separate pots on a bare patio.*

Summer

Some new, dwarf bedding plants such as *Rudbeckia hirta* 'Toto' have already made their mark. Another coneflower is so outstanding that I feel positively deprived if I don't grow it afresh each year. Not only is 'Becky Mixed' likely to outshine all your other daisies, but it also resists the rain well.

BALANCING THE DISPLAY

When initially selecting plants for a project, always ensure that their ultimate height matches the size of your container: a top-heavy container will not only look awkward but may also blow over in a gale. Many sunflowers, *Cosmos* and *Helichrysum* are too large to become widely adopted for use in containers, though on occasions it's fun to plant up a monster pot with something tall and impressive.

Conversely, it is a relief to see bedding *Salvia* getting taller. *S. coccinea* 'Lady in Red'♡ (also a fleuroselect Gold medal winner) is a gem with elegant tiers of bloom and bears little resemblance to the squat pokers of *S. splendens* types such as *S.s.* 'Blaze of Fire'.

△ *Grow on your coleus and coneflowers in pots until they are ready to go into the display bowl.*

◁ *Existing edging plants such as these dead nettles will add instant maturity to newcomers behind.*

▷ *Echo the fiery colours of your coleus leaves by including coneflowers in matching tones in your tabletop harvest festival.*

RECYCLING

Just as a new garden benefits from having one or two mature trees and shrubs, a container with some existing plants is half way to peaking. I have several pots with permanent edges such as these yellow-leaved dead nettles, which almost conceal the bowl, here photographed in late July. When you fancy a change, tidy up the trailers, nipping off any brown leaves and old flower spikes from the dead nettle. Then add fresh potting compost and plants behind.

TOP UP TIME

Coneflowers and coleus can be slow to mature from seed compared to French marigolds or *Cosmos*. Early sown plants should have matured by August, though you don't need to leave it this late to move them into their display pot. Plant the three coneflowers in a triangle, then add the two coleus on either flank. You can almost warm your hands on this pair.

An alternative growplan for the salt-glazed bowl is to plant up the trailing edge of dead nettles and creeping Jenny in April, using young rooted cuttings in plug form or as larger plants in 9cm

OTHER SHADE LOVERS

For flowers *Begonia*, busy lizzies, *Cyclamen*, *Fuchsia*, *Hydrangea*, *Lobelia*, *Nicotiana*, *Rhododendron*, *Sarcococca*, *Viola*

For foliage *Acer*, *Aucuba*, box, *Epimedium*, *Euonymus*, *Fatsia*, *Houttuynia*

Flowers and foliage *Ajuga*, *Astilbe*, *Alchemilla*, *Choisya*, *Helleborus*, *Lamium*, *Mahonia*, *Pieris*, variegated periwinkles

GOOD PLANTS FOR TALL JARS

Clematis alpina♀ and varieties
C. 'Duchess of Albany' ♀
C. x *durandii* ♀
C. florida 'Sieboldii'
Fuchsia 'Golden Marinka' ♀
F. 'Swingtime' ♀
Lotus berthelotii ♀
Petunia Surfinia Series
P. Wave Series 'Pink Wave' and 'Purple Wave'
Scaevola aemula
Tropaeolum Gleam Series
T. 'Jewel of Africa'
T. Whirlybird Series ♀
Verbena 'Pink Parfait'

(3¹/₂in) pots (both are hardy). Then add the young coneflowers and coleus in May and place the bowl in the greenhouse until early June. After that find them a warm, sheltered spot outdoors.

SET THE TABLE

My summer project became the centrepiece for a tabletop harvest festival. My table had a perforated top and I positioned a bowl of water on the smaller, raised circle that holds the legs in place. I then pushed cut flowerheads through the metalwork and their stems into the water below. Visitors were surprised to see how fresh they stayed! I added ripe or fallen fruits to the arrangement as I wandered around the garden.

CONTAINERS FOR SHADE

Many of the most flamboyant, summer-flowering plants will have originated in hot parts of the world: for example *Eschscholzia* comes from California, *Helianthemum* from the Mediterranean and *Gazania* is a native of South Africa. Put them in the shade of trees, walls or fences and they'll just fade away. In fact, some need sun to open their flowers.

When planting containers for shade you need to scale down your expectation of flowers, though if anything a pot-grown *Hosta*, for example, will be far superior to one alongside it in a bed sucked dry by tree roots. All that moist potting compost, regular feeding and relative freedom from slugs and snails does *Hosta* a power of good.

In wet soils and shade, monkey flower

△ *Monkey flowers and variegated* Hosta *will create a colourful spectacle among cool foliage in shaded areas.*

(*Mimulus*) is an invaluable flowerer. It can be grown from seed or bought as named varieties. 'Calypso'♀ – an F₁ hybrid strain with plenty of splashed and speckled blooms – can flower within two months of sowing. There is also a variegated form. I surrounded a *Hosta* 'Wide Brim'♀ with five monkey flowers and, to edge up the salt-glazed bowl, a small-leaved, variegated ivy. Surrounded by a selection of potted ferns, my bowl made a real feature out of what had been a problem site.

▷ *Annual canary creeper* (Tropaeolum perigrinum) *and blue bindweed* (Convolvulus sabatius ♀) *tumble attractively down this tall jar, though the yellow canary creeper will need thinning two or three times if it is not to overrun its partner.*

▷ *Gather your late summer and early autumn forces to create an impressive, banked-up display like this. As one plant fades or is frosted, add another recruit to keep up the momentum.*

Autumn

Even though the year is winding down, there are still plenty of opportunities to breath new life into summer containers by combining them with some of the earliest autumn-colouring shrubs and climbers as well as one or two specials.

The idea of grouping individual containers to make a lavish showpiece occurs frequently in this book. Not only do they look better but you'll also find they protect each other, a fact borne out by reduced water loss. Bare tarmac drives, ugly concrete slabs and stark brickwork can readily be transformed in a couple of hours.

BUILDING A FRAME

Not everyone wants to smother their house in climbers and wall shrubs. They might for example be worried about all that training and tying in the wisteria or climbing roses will demand. An easy way to build up a really impressive bank of colour is to use a container-grown climber or wall shrub. Painted walls are perhaps the best background to

△ *I started off with an existing potted ornamental grape vine (Vitis coignetiae♡) as my key plant to anchor the autumn showpiece to its surroundings.*

offset bright colours, so that you avoid that potential mismatch of red bricks with orange and red flowers.

△ *Who needs flowers, when autumn foliage alone can look this good?*

In my autumn project, I have placed two key pots right in the foreground. My *Pelargonium* trio used three of the best foliage varieties: 'Frank Headley'♀ (an absolute gem with sage-green-and-white leaves and pink flowers); 'Madame Salleron'♀ (which never flowers for me) and 'Crystal Palace Gem' (also a gem with yellow-margined leaves and brilliant red blooms). To the right of this trio is the cabbage bowl, which is filled with even more spectacular foliage.

Behind my two leading pots I filled in with more bedding plants such as busy lizzies, purple *Salvia*, pansies and *Lobelia*. None of these would win prizes on their own but en masse they looked a treat. Some pots of *Crocosmia* 'Solfatare' were positioned under the grape vine so their flowers really shone out. I finished the display with a touch of grey and yellow.

CABBAGES ARE KING
I showed off a bit by planting ornamental cabbage 'Tokyo Mixed' with the sought-after, variegated spurge, 'Burrow Silver', which I bought at a national gardening show – the perfect venue to pick up good introductions. Still on a foliage theme I squeezed into the salt-glazed bowl some foot-loose *Houttuynia* (which spreads like mint so it's safer in a container) and to edge and trail a yellow-veined clover. The display lasted for weeks.

Winter

The seasonal indicator for this recipe will probably have you rubbing your eyes in disbelief: seven months of interest from one pot and much of it through winter? It can be done if you seek out plants that look as good in bud as in flower.

You're probably familiar with *Skimmia japonica* 'Rubella', a male form whose conspicuous, red flower buds develop in late summer but wait until the following spring to open. Young plants are particularly impressive in their size and quantity of flower. Imported specimens have three young plants per pot (like the one here) so you get dense, well-rounded specimens. *Pieris* are naturally rounded and 'Cupido' also has red buds and is well worth seeking out.

LIME HATERS
None of these plants likes lime, so half fill the salt-glazed bowl with ericaceous potting compost, then plant the *Pieris*. Add the *Skimmia*, packing in more compost between the rootballs, then raise the compost level for the bud heathers. The buds of these fascinating plants never actually open although they remain colourful for months.

The long-awaited *Skimmia* and *Pieris* blossom emerges in the following March and April. I think I prefer the *Skimmia* in bud, even though the flowers do smell good. You can always add pots of scented wallflowers and polyanthus for more fragrance. After flowering, move the plants into individual pots to grow on or plant them out in a bed as the basis of a winter garden.

△ *The* Skimmia *and* Pieris *buds will eventually open into flowers, in spring, by which time the heather will be past its prime.*

◁ *The warming, red buds of* Skimmia *will glow for months on end during winter.*

Small Terracotta Pans

Traditional terracotta pans and pots are perfect for tiny, alpine treasures that may hidden in the open garden. Such containers also allow you to raise the plants to eye level. Being porous, they let plant roots breathe and because they dry out more quickly than plastic you are less likely to overwater plants prone to rotting.

LARGE PAN	MEDIUM PAN	SMALL PAN
Height	Height	Height
15cm (6in)	12.5cm (5in)	7.5cm (3in)
Diameter	Diameter	Diameter
25cm (10in)	25cm (10in)	15cm (6in)
Weight	Weight	Weight
2kg (4½lb)	1kg (2lb)	0.5kg (1lb)

Spring

Small pans and pots are invaluable in springtime and are particularly effective when used for a simple arrangement, although I'm not a great fan of single species pots. I'd rather buy one large container and weave all the plants together. However a grouped collection of *Crocus*, *Viola* or primroses in small pots can be a delight if you prepare a special setting. There are several such little theatres on view in the next few pages.

CLASSIC PAIRING

Having two spring dazzlers in an intimate embrace really does emphasise how well they work together in a bed or pan. Glory of the snow is a precocious bulb. Not as blue as Siberian squill (*Scilla sibirica*♥) maybe, but once glory of the snow has decided to open its flowers, they stay open and quickly form starry carpets, impervious to the elements. (Some bulbs wait for the sun before opening their flowers.) Its perfect partner is *Arabis blepharophylla* 'Frühlingszauber'.

Plant up the large pan in autumn with the *Arabis* in a well-drained, gritty compost mix. Top up with more gritty compost before pushing in the glory of the snow bulbs. Finish off with a topdressing of grit or fine gravel to improve drainage around the necks of the *Arabis*.

Position the pan on a stone slab and surround it with a rock or two, infilling with gravel to make a mountainscape for your pan.

AURICULA ARENA

I think you'll be captivated by this magic mix of dwarf wallflowers and auricula primroses. All those extrovert colours in weathered pots scenting the air delight the eye and the nose! Auriculas do very well in pots. In fact, that's

△ *Simple ideas are often the best. The glory of the snow and pink* Arabis *here make a perfect pair.*

△ *Dwarf wallflowers and auriculas make a classic perfumed partnership that oozes cottage-garden charm.*

exactly how the most sought-after, perfectly-formed show varieties are grown.

These are not prize winners but border auriculas, which have a more informal, fancy-free personality. You can buy them in flower in spring, picking out the colours you like, or grow them from seed, which is more haphazard. If you're really smitten, go to a specialist show and select some of those incredible black or green, named varieties. You will however have to cultivate them in a cool greenhouse.

Grow your dwarf wallflowers (such as *Erysimum cheiri* 'Tom Thumb Mixed') from seed sown in May or June or buy a bareroot bundle in autumn and pot them up. Mulch the pots and display area with small Cotswold limestone chippings – wallflowers and auriculas love lime and slugs hate to cross sharp-edged chippings.

▷ *A substantial garden seat or bench can quickly form a tiered display stand for your favourite plants.*

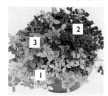
Summer

A little forethought is needed before planting up such small containers as these pans with hyperactive *Petunia* or thirsty busy lizzies. Tall plants will also look top-heavy and it's a shame to conceal mellow terracotta with vigorous trailing plants.

LUCKY CLOVER

Some say that you make your own luck, and if so I should be a very lucky man because I planted a pot of four-leaved clovers, which on occasions even produced five leaves. When I forgot to water it for a week, it survived – though clover in lawns does stay green long after the grass has turned brown.

For my summer display I mixed three foliage plants: two ornamental clovers and shamrock. The latter is often sold as dry bulbs in spring or as a potted plant. Clovers are sold as plugs or young plants. Pot them up in April and by mid-summer you should start to see the flowers; the yellow-veined clover has pale rose blooms, the purple-leaved clover has white and the shamrock's are a lovely shade of pink.

△ *Gardeners who consider clover and shamrock to be weeds will be pleasantly surprised by this trio.*

SUCCULENT SCENES

When you move your windowsill succulents into the garden in summer, why not transplant them from their individual pots into a more spacious terracotta pan? They'll more than double in size in a season. Rosette-forming varieties such as these *Echeveria* and *Haworthia* look impressive when viewed from above so these two pans were set alongside a stepping-stone-and-gravel path.

To achieve a contrast in colour and texture and to fill in between the more sizeable types, fleshy-leaved varieties of alpines such as stonecrop (*Sedum*) and houseleeks (*Sempervivum*) are invaluable. Group your succulent pans together for the best effect. Three of contrasting diameters and heights is the classic arrangement.

OTHER GOOD PLANTS FOR TERRACOTTA PANS

alpine and cottage pinks
chamomile
Felicea amelloides 'Variegata'
Gazania
Helianthemum
houseleek
Sedum spathulifolium 'Purpureum' ♀
thyme

◁ *Hardy, fleshy-leaved alpines planted beside tender, rosette-shaped succulents bring out the best of these shallow pans.*

Autumn

Falling temperatures and shortening days trigger the flowering mechanism in some bulbs. They then seed and die down before the worst of the weather sets in. Such is the case with the tiny autumn-flowering *Crocus*, which may look frail but in shallow pans really shines out. This is the true *Crocus*, in no way related to *Colchicum*, which frequently shares the same common name.

MATCHMAKING

In August I ordered some autumn-flowering *Crocus* from a specialist supplier, who keeps the bulbs in a cold store to extend the planting season. Some may even flower in transit. I potted up my bulbs on the day they arrived (2 October) and they were in full bloom about a month later.

For suitable partners, search no further than these chemically dwarfed michaelmas daisies. For a foil, the leaves of *Cyclamen hederifolium* are ideal and this plant is quite happy in a terracotta pan.

▽ *For my collection of* Crocus, Cyclamen *and michaelmas daisies I made a tiered display stand from blue Victorian pavers, rope-top edgings and broken ceramic tiles. It looked lovely in the fading autumn sunlight.*

AUTUMN RECIPE

JAN	FEB	MAR	APR	MAY	JUN
JUL	AUG	SEP	OCT	NOV	DEC

YOU WILL NEED

- 12 white autumn *Crocus* (*C. pulchellus* 'Zephyr' ♀) (1)
- 6 lilac autumn *Crocus* (*C. medius* ♀) (2)
- 12 pale lavender blue autumn *Crocus* (*C. speciosus* 'Artabir') (3)
- 4 dwarf michaelmas daisies (dwarfed *Aster novi-belgii* varieties) (4)
- 1 *Cyclamen hederifolium* ♀ (5)
- broken polystyrene chunks or crocks
- 5 litres multipurpose potting compost
- fine gravel for topdressing *Crocus* pans

Winter

Some autumn *Crocus* may still be in flower at the same time as the earliest, true winter-flowering species begin to bloom if grown in a warm border against a wall. The advantage of cultivating these sparkling jewels in pots and pans is that you can bring them into a porch, conservatory or greenhouse and force them on a little.

Plant your *Crocus* bulbs in clay pots in autumn. The smaller-flowered types tend to bloom earlier than the larger-flowered, robust, Dutch hybrids, so if you want a spread of flowers choose some from each group. *C. tommasinianus* ♀ is among the first to show, followed by varieties of *C. chrysanthus*. A mixture of purple, pale lilac and yellow always look good. Snip off spent flowers once they spill forward over the container rims and begin to shrivel up. You can keep these bulbs in pots for a repeat performance or plant them out and try new varieties each year.

◁ Crocus *never look better than when clustered together in small terracotta pots and pans in winter.*

WINTER RECIPE

JAN	FEB	MAR	APR	MAY	JUN
JUL	AUG	SEP	OCT	NOV	DEC

YOU WILL NEED

- 10 *Crocus tommasinianus* 'Whitewell Purple' (1)
- 10 winter *Crocus* (*C. chrysanthus* var. *fuscotinctus*) (2)
- 10 Dutch hybrid *Crocus* (*C. vernus* 'Purpureus Grandiflorus') (3)
- 10 *C. sieberi* 'Tricolor' ♀ (4)
- broken polystyrene chunks or crocks
- 5 litres multipurpose potting compost
- moss for topdressing

JAN	FEB	MAR	APR	MAY	JUN
JUL	AUG	SEP	OCT	NOV	DEC

YOU WILL NEED

- 20 scented, double daffodils (*Narcissus* 'Bridal Crown') (1)
- 20 blue grape hyacinths (*Muscari armeniacum* ♀) (2)
- 3 yellow-leaved feverfew (*Tanacetum parthenium* 'Aureum') (3)
- hessian or hay for lining the basket
- 16 litres multipurpose potting compost for the pots inside the basket

GOOD SUBSTITUTES

Instead of daffodils try white hyacinths in pots as they come into flower.

FOR CONTINUITY

As my 'Bridal Crown' daffodils outlasted the grape hyacinths, I replaced the grape hyacinths with pink *Anemone coronaria* De Caen Group and blue *A. blanda* ♀ plus a sprinkling of pansies, as you'll see opposite.

ALTERNATIVELY

Grape hyacinths, although common, are tough, reliable, inexpensive and ideal for containers that need an early injection of blue (see page 128).

Large Willow Basket

Shopping baskets make excellent planters. To prolong their lifespan stitch in plastic liners, paint each basket with three coats of clear preservative or yacht varnish, and move to a sheltered spot in winter. Even though home-produced baskets such as this tend to be stronger than imported ones, don't hang them by their handle.

Height 20cm (8in)
Width 30cm (12in)
Length 50cm (20in)
Weight 2kg (4½lb)

Spring

It is in spring, perhaps, that woven baskets look most appealing, lending a charming country flavour to displays of bulbs, bedding and early cottage-garden perennials. Much of this atmosphere will be lost if you position your basket on a white plastic table or bare paving. Try it instead on a pathway alongside a border, nestling in among other wicker or wooden containers or rising up out of a haze of forget-me-nots or bluebells. If you live in a country cottage, bring it onto a window ledge or put it on a shelf beneath a window where you can enjoy the flowers and perfume.

ADVANCE PLANNING

Double-flowered daffodils such as these tazetta hybrids produce a welcome abundance of long-lasting bloom and exude a heavenly scent. You'll need to order them from a specialist nursery and pot them up in autumn because you're unlikely to find them for sale in spring. Grape hyacinths should also be potted up in autumn. Golden feverfew you need buy only once; it seeds itself without becoming a nuisance. These three were dug up from a border in March.

CRAM A BASKET

There's no point in leaving room for expansion in these spring arrangements because bulbs won't spread. Line the basket with a thick layer of hay or a piece of hessian sacking and insert the daffodils first, leaving them in their pots if you wish. Potted bulbs are more convenient to replant in a border after flowering, though you'll need to hide the rims with more hay. I folded my overhanging hessian liner back inside for an instant cover-up. Also try and envelop the handle so it doesn't separate the bulbs from the rest of the planting.

Work the grape hyacinths through the feverfew so they are thrown into sharp focus and angle them to spill over the basket rim. It looks a treat and will work just as well in a bed or border.

▷ Keep up the momentum by replacing spent plants with new ones as soon as they go over.

▽ Advance planning pays dividends when you produce a basket brimming with spring flowers such as these.

◁ Pack the daffodil bulbs in tightly as they do not need space in which to develop.

YOU WILL NEED

- 9 annual *Phlox* (*P. drummondii* 'Phlox of Sheep') in 9cm (3½in) pots or three each in three 13cm (5in) pots (1)
- 1 tray Swan river daisies (*Brachyscome iberidifolia* 'Bravo Mixed') (2)
- hay for lining the basket, with a plastic liner beneath
- 20 litres multipurpose potting compost

△ *For strong contrasts, try Swan river daisies with these vibrant orange, seed-raised* Ursinia *daisies and red* Verbena.

GOOD SUBSTITUTES

Try *Verbena* 'Pink Parfait' with red-and-white striped, single or double *Petunia*, or *P.* 'Purple Wave' with yellow, trailing *Bidens*. *Tropaeolum* Alaska Series ♀ goes well with dwarf sunflower *Helianthus* 'Pacino', as does *Tagetes* 'Vanilla' with blue *Scaevola aemula*.

Summer

There's nothing like a gimmick to get sales of seeds and plants really moving, and I and many thousands of others were attracted to the name 'Phlox of Sheep'. Each year I aim to try something new and as almost anything will grow in a pot why should I restrict my horticultural horizons to *Pelargonium*, *Fuchsia*, busy lizzies and trailing *Lobelia*? Thus I discovered that 'Phlox of Sheep' and Swan river daisies are made for each other.

Both the tender perennial and annual Swan river daisies have the same wiry stems and wandering habit, which is eager to spill over a pot edge. They mix with almost any colour, too. Many annual *Phlox* also look good toppling over the edge of small containers.

GET SOWING

Gardeners who don't sow seed miss out on some of the really interesting plants that never make it onto the bedding sales benches. If you avoid sowing because you dislike pricking out, try spacing out the seeds in the seed tray and letting them grow on to planting size. Alternatively sow three or four seeds in cell trays so you have a plug to work with. Such advice is fine as long as the seeds are not too tiny to handle.

In March I sprinkled about 60 Swan river daisy seeds over a seed tray and just over three months later they proved to be the best mixture I'd seen. Planting out is best achieved by transferring the daisy 'turf' to the display basket. It also works well with *Nemesia*. This method is far better than tearing the 'turf' up into individual plants with all the root damage that would result when seedlings are this far advanced.

By June 'Phlox of Sheep' was also beginning to reveal its delicate nature with pastel pinks and buffs (some with perfume), from a March sowing. I transplanted it into 13cm (5in) pots, three plants to a pot, then in early July into the basket where it began to trail attractively – so much so that I had to raise the basket onto an upturned flowerpot in a convenient gap in a flowering border.

△ *Don't feel guilty if you forget to prick out your Swan river daisies. Sow seed thinly over a seed tray and you'll end up with thick daisy turf that can be dropped straight into the display basket.*

◁ *Allow* Phlox *to trail over the edge of the basket if it starts to wander like this.*

Autumn

Many summer bedding plants begin to look tired by late August, especially if they've dried out a couple of times, have set seed or naturally have a short season. To take their place why not fill your willow basket with perky autumnal flowers and colourful foliage plants. Start in early September, when all the plants are readily available. With the addition of dwarf bulbs, this plant collection will provide the framework for a winter and spring showpiece. The ingredients can be bought from a garden centre or nursery and will look good soon after they are planted.

When you are choosing plants for a border, there are many things to consider – both practical and aesthetic. With container gardening it's much simpler because you exercise control over the growing conditions (soil, sun and exposure), leaving you free to be creative – hence its popularity.

TRIAL RUN

There's no better way to get a feel for successful plant associations than to gather up a selection of seasonal varieties and move them around on the floor to see how they work together. Purple and yellow are complementary colours so a purple cabbage will look richer against yellow foliage than a white one. Ruddy-leaved *Leucothoe* is backlit by the same yellow tree heather. The upper pansy petals pick up this deep red, while their faces reflect the yellow. The ivy weaving through the basket pulls it all together. Dwarf bulbs add the continuity.

PLANTING UP

Line the basket with black plastic sheeting. A cut-up compost bag, black side facing outwards, is ideal. Make a few slits in the base, then cover it with a layer of ericaceous compost (the heather and *Leucothoe* dislike lime). Position the heather then the *Leucothoe* and cabbage. Angle all three plants towards the front and fill in between their rootballs with more compost. Tuck in the ivy and direct it sideways along the front edge, over the sides

△ *Winter pansies and spring bulbs will provide the floral contribution to a basket of evergreens with contrasting growth habits and colours.*

and across the handle if the trails are long enough. Finish off with the pansies.

Spray off any spilt compost and spend a few minutes carefully dressing the plants. Reveal the pansies by teasing out their blooms from the surrounding foliage.

▷ *Contrast is the key to achieving a lively planting scheme. This autumnal selection will also provide the framework for winter too.*

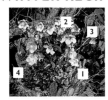
▷ *Plant out the Lenten roses in May in front of a yellow-flowered* Mahonia japonica ♀. *Include the red* Leucothoe *from the large willow basket with yellow-variegated* Euonymus, *winter heathers, pink* Gaultheria *and orange* Crocus ancyrensis.

△ *Once the Lenten roses are well positioned, add the twiggy 'crutches' to support their flower heads.*

Winter

No matter how hard you try, you'll never quite match the intensity of summer's torrent of flowers in the dead of winter. Apart from winter heathers, few plants have the sheer weight of bloom to attract attention. You may only realise that some, such as *Sarcococca* and *Azara microphylla* ♀, are in flower when you detect their tell-tale perfume scenting the air.

Winter interest is more spread out, on the young twigs of witch hazel (*Hamamelis*) and *Viburnum* branches, for example, or captured in ripe berries or coloured twigs. To appreciate this subtle beauty you need to highlight it in a sheltered, sunny spot, preferably near a house window or door for effortless viewing.

FLOWER SUPPORT

Imagine how your outlook would improve if you could gaze on the upturned faces of these Lenten roses at a time when other gardeners have to content themselves with thumbing the seed catalogues and longing for summer. They really do bring winter cheer. If you prop up the flowers with coloured twigs to let the slanting, watery sunlight explore their faces and add a few companion plants below, then your willow basket will look much like mine.

Start off with two or three hand-picked Lenten rose hybrids and position them at the back of the basket, feeding some flower stalks up in front of the handle before the pots are in position. Fill in around the pots with hay. Not only does this hide the plastic rims but it is also a good insulator against frost. Cut some stiff, red or yellow twigs from willow or dogwood. Push the thick ends into the Lenten rose rootball and use the V-shaped tips as crutches to ease up the nodding flowers. Fill in with other seasonal plants, add more hay to steady them and finish off with an edging of fir cones – though not if you want to deter squirrels.

△ *These 'Ashwood Hybrid' Lenten roses are a superb strain with about 15 different flower colours. February is the best time to buy them as you can see exactly what you're getting. Although the flowers become more pendulous as they age, the angle they tilt varies so look for ones that give you a glimpse of their stamens.*

▷ *Find a sheltered, sunny spot in which to place your winter basket and spend five minutes a day admiring your handiwork.*

SPRING RECIPE

| JAN | FEB | MAR | APR | MAY | JUN |
| JUL | AUG | SEP | OCT | NOV | DEC |

YOU WILL NEED

- 2 stinking hellebore (*Helleborus foetidus* 'Wester Flisk') (1)
- 4 pink-and-yellow primroses (*Primula vulgaris*) (2)
- 2 blue *Anemone blanda* ♥ (3)
- broken polystyrene chunks or crocks
- 20 litres multipurpose potting compost

GOOD SUBSTITUTES

Corsican hellebore (*Helleborus argutifolius* ♥) or *H. lividus* ♥ are perhaps even more desirable though not quite as tough as the stinker.

ALTERNATIVELY

Stinking hellebore is used in a very different role on page 139.

Terracotta Urn

Urns come in all materials, shapes, sizes and depths and this one is deep enough to support a rich variety of plants. The base usually separates from the bowl, making it easier to transport and set up in a border. Wrap imported terracotta like this in hessian in severe weather or accept that a bit of surface damage will add to the character of the urn.

Height (including base)
63cm (25in)
Diameter 40cm (16in)
Weight 26kg (57lb)

Spring

An urn adds a touch of formality to a setting, although you don't have to site it or plant it in a formal, regimented way. This spring gathering has a real woodland feel about it. Generally, it's best to steer clear of the taller varieties of daffodils and tulips because, raised up in an urn, they will be prone to buffeting winds and there's just not room to support them with bushy evergreens.

FOCAL POINT

It takes a leap in imagination to picture your urn as an irresistible focal point in a border rather than on a patio, but it's worth the effort because it will be surrounded by a flattering backdrop of flowers and foliage. I set mine in front of a plum that flowered at primrose time and provided a dramatic backcloth of purple foliage when it was the tulips' turn. The key plant that remained through both scene changes was 'Wester Flisk' stinking hellebore, with its red stems and leaf stalks. It looks good for months. Try it with a border of blue *Anemone* and pink-and-yellow primroses.

△ *Fill out the base of your hellebore display with pots of flowering primroses and* Anemone.

KEEP IT GOING

The ability to think ahead brings rich rewards for the aspiring non-stop container gardener. In November I potted up ten early double 'Fringed Beauty' tulips, so that by spring I could dream up some mouth-watering bulb and bedding duos. The yellow, frilly petal edges of the tulips were picked up by Bowles' golden grass (*Milium effusum* 'Aureum') at the front, itself a contrast with the blue-green tulip leaves. The *Anemone* and primroses that were previously in the pot had meanwhile been planted out on the edge of a woodland bed, where they settled in well. Nothing goes to waste in my garden.

◁ *Keep your urn at fever pitch in spring by topping up with pot-grown 'Fringed Beauty' tulips and Bowles' golden grass.*

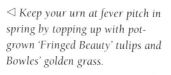

▷ *Open up a whole new world by siting your urn in a border – but make sure you have access for maintenance and adding new plants.*

| JAN | FEB | MAR | APR | MAY | JUN |
| JUL | AUG | SEP | OCT | NOV | DEC |

YOU WILL NEED
- 5 pink 'Love Duet' pansies (1)
- 2 lambs' lugs (*Stachys byzantina*) (2)
- broken polystyrene chunks or crocks
- 20 litres multipurpose potting compost

GOOD SUBSTITUTES
For a non-flowering form of *Stachys* try *S. byzantina* 'Silver Carpet'. *S.b.* 'Primrose Heron' is unusual, with yellow-hued leaves, especially in spring.

FOR CONTINUITY
Regular deadheading will keep your pansies constantly in bloom although some varieties react badly to the heat and quickly grow straggly and unkempt. Replace these with dwarf *Aster* such as these 'Teisa Stars'.

ALTERNATIVELY
For other pansy combinations for early summer see page 67.

▷ *The two-tone pansy flowers with their rich raspberry-rose centres are diluted by grey-leaved lambs' lugs and the pastel colours behind the urn.*

Summer

Some urns rely on shape rather than decoration to make their mark. My Grecian urn is more extrovert with an egg-and-dart pattern around the rim and swags of fruit on the bowl. Although it's a shame to hide such detail, it's also a pity to deprive yourself of all those sensational summer trailers. If I had the self-control, I could have planted this urn with a single species, say an ornamental grass like blue fescue or a tighter sward of box cut 5–7.5cm (2–3in) high for a contemporary feel. I wanted a more flowery, romantic picture, however.

SUPPORTING CAST

I'm a restless gardener and nothing in my garden stays the same for long. The urn was transported to another sunny border in May where I was expecting a bumper crop of flowers from a *Clematis* and *Ceanothus* pairing. Up went the urn and I put in a mixture of dark pink-faced pansies and grey foliage. I selected 'Love Duet', a pansy with a raspberry-rose centre on a white background. You may prefer those with a suffusion of pink over the whole flower with darker blotches and whiskers like 'Pink Panther'.

OVERCOMING OBSTACLES

It's so easy to be intimidated by gardening rules about when is the perfect time to transplant this or that. Fortunately most container-grown plants transplanted into beds and borders start life with a pre-formed, pot-shaped ball of roots. If they are moved, even after a year or two, this rootball should still remain intact. The plant should also re-establish well, even during the growing season, and especially if – like these lamb's lugs – it's been moved from a border to a pot, where perfect growing conditions can be provided.

RAMPANT PLANTS

African marigolds are flowers that fashion-conscious gardeners love to hate especially now that *Dahlia* have become more popular and even on occasions achieved cult status. (No red border is complete without 'Bishop of Llandaff' for example.) Big blobs of unrestrained African marigold orange create a zingy, fresh and sharp impact in a nest of silver and white foliage and flowers, while seed-raised *Brachyscome* and *Petunia* are the perfect accompaniment.

The silver-leaved *Artemisia ludoviciana* 'Valerie Finnis'♀ proved too rampant and the young seedling *Eucalyptus* seemed like a good idea at the time, but both proved to be just too boisterous and choked out the flowers in the urn. You can learn from my mistakes and it was good while it lasted.

◁ *Although the colour scheme has much to commend it, a more manageable, silver-leaved plant such as* Tanacetum ptarmiciflorum Silver Feather *would ensure success.*

▽ *A cluster of cabbage palms is guaranteed to create an eye-catching vista in your garden.*

CORDYLINE CORNER

There's no risk when you opt for cabbage palms (*Cordyline*) as urn fillers. They have a classic symmetry that makes them perhaps the finest plants of all to lend a formal appearance to an urn. They also work well in chimney pots. If you are planning to frame a doorway be sure to pick out two cabbage palms that are well matched and of the same variety.

Bear in mind that variegated and purple varieties need protection over winter; even the green *C. australis*♀ can lose its growing tip as a youngster in severe weather. Purple- and bronze-leaved forms need yellow or variegated leaves behind them or they may get overlooked.

Cabbage palms are greedy and can double in size in a season so, around the base, tuck in tough plants such as these brilliant red *Pelargonium*, succulent-leaved *Echeveria* and, if you can seek it out, the scrumptious, variegated *Sedum alboroseum* 'Mediovariegatum'. Be warned though. Vine weevil beetles will go to great lengths (and heights) to locate the *Sedum*.

Autumn

Given a relatively frost-free autumn, there's no reason why long-flowering, summer bedding plants such as busy lizzies, French marigolds and nasturtiums shouldn't rub shoulders with late starters such as chrysanths, pink *Nerine* and Japanese maples.

The best way to do this is to freshen up an existing container by digging out the spent plants, adding fresh compost and then laying on a double helping of colour. You don't even have to plant out these dwarf chrysanths. Their pots can be tucked among the summer foliage – but don't forget to water them or the secret will be out.

REFRESHER COURSE

One way to get instant maturity in a new container is to transplant a sizeable trailer from another pot, in this case the tumbling, grey-leaved *Hebe* at the front. Since spring it has threaded its way through more ephemeral planting, making a great foil for blue grape hyacinths and now pink busy lizzies. Another first-rate weaver is *Leucothoe* with its flashy variegation that takes on plum and bronze tints before the year is out.

Once the chrysanth is in place, direct a few white-speckled *Leucothoe* shoots up into its blooms. The *Leucothoe* and *Hebe* will give you a flying start for your winter scheme, unless you prefer purple hellebores rising out of yellow foliage (see below).

△ *This blend of autumn foliage and flowers is subtle yet showy.*

Winter

Winter gardening can be a letdown if you're on a shoestring budget, because you'll miss out on some of the most juicy plants. I splashed out on this red-berried *Skimmia* but it repaid me with over six months of non-stop, glowing berry colour. The birds didn't seem to notice it at all.

LEAF HIGHLIGHTS

Euonymus fortunei 'Emerald 'n' Gold' not only nudges up the nodding heads of the Lenten rose a little but also highlights their dark blooms and the red *Skimmia* berries, as well as billowing out to soften the rim of the urn. That's a big job for one plant, so use two bushy ones – they can be quite variable in their habit of growth so choose carefully.

The Lenten rose was bought the previous winter and, after flowering, potted up into a larger container to grow on. Such a sizeable rootball takes up the lion's share of the urn, which is another reason why you need to fill in with plants such as *Euonymus* that grow extensively from a relatively compact rootball and disguise the bare soil if you angle them in the right direction.

◁ *Highlight Lenten roses in winter by planting them above yellow foliage plants such as* Euonymus fortunei *'Emerald 'n' Gold'.*

▷ *By autumn, my terracotta urn was almost submerged in foliage and flowers above and a carpet of blue juniper at its feet.*

Galvanised Tin Bath

There was a time when tin baths like this would have been seen hanging up in every backyard waiting for washday (or even bathnight). They now have other uses as their oval shape, width and depth allow you to grow almost anything you fancy, as long as you drill plenty of drainage holes in the base.

Height 23cm (9in)
Width 45cm (18in)
Length 58cm (23in)
Weight 5kg (11lb)

Spring

Do I detect a movement away from those traditional alpine rock gardens banked up with tons of stone? The extraction of water-worn limestone from areas of great natural beauty has certainly deterred conservation-minded gardeners. Alpines in containers though have never been more popular.

ALPINE CARPET

Although not all the plants here are true alpines, they do nevertheless light up the patio from March to May. All can be bought in spring in bloom. The red-berried, lime-hating *Gaultheria* and dwarf cypress were moved in early March from a winter arrangement to the tin bath. I potted the *Anemone* in autumn to be sure of getting pink ones. At the same time, I planted the double daisies in a border and transferred them to the bath in March.

△ *Grow your alpines in containers so that you can control the soil conditions and aspect.*

Summer

Of all the gardens I've designed and maintained, the ones that have given me greatest pleasure are ornamental kitchen gardens, a mouth-watering blend of the decorative and productive. There's no reason why you can't achieve the 'potager' look in a few containers. If anything, the plants grow even better. It's also fun to add a utilitarian character by planting in tin buckets and baths. By early August, mine was almost completely hidden beneath a feast of tender leaves, pods and vibrant flowers.

SEEDS AND PLANTS

With this recipe, it's a good idea to share seedlings with your gardening friends because you need only one red cabbage. Sow the cabbage in March, the pot marigolds in April and the ruby chard in May in a cold frame or greenhouse. Sowing too early or transplanting can cause ruby chard to run to seed, so sow two seeds in each compartment of a cell tray and you will be able to move these small plugs to their tin bath without root disturbance. Add a clump of yellow marjoram dug from a border or three small, pot-grown plants. By early to mid-June everything should be in place.

△ *Surround a yellow marjoram with Oxalis tetraphylla 'Iron Cross', Geranium cinereum 'Ballerina' ♀, Hebe 'Margret' and the brightest red rock rose you can lay hands on. This is Helianthemum 'Ben Ledi'.*

▷ *With your tin bath as the centrepiece, add dwarf beans, parsley, marigolds and sweetcorn. It's a feast for the senses.*

Autumn

At the merest mention of autumn leaves you may be instantly transported to the maple glade at Westonbirt Arboretum or to lakeside panoramas at Sheffield Park where sweet gums perform a double act, once on land and once reflected on the water surface. It's a shame to be wishing the year away however as some foliage plants are still around that bear only the slightest hint of those terminal tints. If you're clever you can even work some summer trailers such as nasturtiums into your creation as well.

THE MAGNIFICENT SEVEN

All my magnificent seven for autumn are outstanding container plants, though none is perfect. Ornamental cabbage and kale are not totally hardy, *Houttuynia* can outmanoeuvre mint, slugs eat *Hosta*, bugles can become mildewed, double nasturtiums can be hard to overwinter and golden marjoram can scorch in hot sun.

◁ *A little time spent trying to understand your plants' needs is well worthwhile as they will reward you with an outpouring of foliage and flowers as impressive as this autumn display.*

AUTUMN LEAVES

Start off with three contrasting brassicas: feather types and 'Red Peacock' have lacy, fern-like leaves in white or purple; 'Red Chidori' and 'Nagoya Mixed' have curly edges; and Northern Lights Series have centres like blowsy peonies. Space them out and fill in with *Hosta*, ringed around with *Houttuynia*. These two contrast well with the cabbage and kale leaves. Add your summer trailer and thread it around the foliage plants. Finally fill any gaps with marjoram and purple-leaved bugle.

Sheltered under a house wall, this planting should still flourish through November, but bring the nasturtium indoors if frost is forecast.

AUTUMN RECIPE

JAN	FEB	MAR	APR	MAY	JUN
JUL	AUG	SEP	OCT	NOV	DEC

YOU WILL NEED

- 2 'Red Peacock' ornamental kale (1)
- 1 'Red Chidori' ornamental kale (2)
- 1 Northern Lights Series ornamental cabbage (3)
- 1 *Hosta* 'June' (4)
- 2 *Houttuynia* 'Joseph's Coat' (5)
- 1 double nasturtium (*Tropaeolum majus* 'Hermine Grashoff' ♀) (6)
- 1 golden marjoram (*Origanum vulgare* 'Aureum' ♀) (7)
- 1 purple-leaved bugle (*Ajuga reptans* 'Catlin's Giant' ♀) (8)
- broken polystyrene chunks or crocks
- 40 litres multipurpose potting compost

△ *One big specimen or two smaller cotton lavenders, filling out the back of your winter tin bath, might conjure up memories of snow on a mountain peak.*

Winter

'Red Peacock' kale is perhaps the hardiest of the ornamental varieties partly because kale is by nature tougher than cabbage and also, I suspect, because its leaves shed rain. Use the two kale from the autumn tin bath to set up a pink and purple colour scheme for the winter months. It's worth increasing the depth of drainage material now so that the compost doesn't waterlog.

PINKS AND PURPLES

For something a bit different why not create a soft pink and purple colour theme set against a foil of grey foliage, which picks up the galvanised container. There's a good range of plants to choose from including most winter heathers. If you're impatient for colour, 'Kramer's Rote' is among the first heathers to bloom and its extra long spikes make it a bestseller.

Pernettyas too with pink and purple berries look good at the front of a display and will last well into spring, but you will also need a male plant to ensure berries next year.

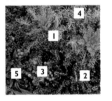

WINTER RECIPE

JAN	FEB	MAR	APR	MAY	JUN
JUL	AUG	SEP	OCT	NOV	DEC

YOU WILL NEED

- 2 'Red Peacock' ornamental kale (1)
- 2 mature winter heathers (*Erica* x *darleyensis* 'Kramer's Rote' ♀, syn. 'Kramer's Red') (2)
- 1 female, pink pernettya (*Gaultheria mucronata* ♀) (3)
- 1 or 2 cotton lavenders (*Santolina pinnata* subsp. *neapolitana* ♀) (4)
- 1 *Leucothoe* 'Scarletta' (5)
- broken polystyrene chunks or crocks
- 40 litres ericaceous (lime-free) potting compost

Wooden Tubs

These wooden tubs are made for plants, unlike half barrels which assumed this role in the garden when brewers replaced them with aluminium casks. Three of the hardwood staves extend below the bottom metal hoop to make short feet. Such tubs are better insulated than terracotta and retain moisture longer.

LARGE TUB	MEDIUM TUB	SMALL TUB
Height	Height	Height
35cm (14in)	30cm (12in)	25cm (10in)
Diameter	Diameter	Diameter
40cm (16in)	35cm (14in)	30cm (12in)
Weight	Weight	Weight
8kg (18lb)	7kg (15lb)	5kg (11lb)

SPRING RECIPE

JAN	FEB	MAR	APR	MAY	JUN
JUL	AUG	SEP	OCT	NOV	DEC

YOU WILL NEED

- 10 'February Silver' daffodils ♀ (1)
- 10 'Delft Blue' hyacinths ♀ (2)
- 10 'Prins Hendrik' hyacinths (3)
- broken polystyrene chunks or crocks
- 20 litres multipurpose potting compost

ALTERNATIVELY

For more ways to get the most from hyacinths see page 122.

▷ *In spring, prop up some of the lanky hyacinths with tree prunings.*

SUMMER RECIPE

JAN	FEB	MAR	APR	MAY	JUN
JUL	AUG	SEP	OCT	NOV	DEC

YOU WILL NEED

- 2 double, red, variegated busy lizzies (*Impatiens* 'Dapper Dan') (1)
- 2 *Houttuynia* 'Joseph's Coat' (2)
- 5 Prince of Wales feathers (*Celosia argentea* 'New Look') (3)
- 1 *Fuchsia* 'Thalia' ♀ (4)
- broken polystyrene chunks or crocks
- 20 litres multipurpose potting compost

GOOD SUBSTITUTES

Red Snapdragons such as *Antirrhinum majus* 'Black Prince' can be used instead of the *Celosia* and red love-lies-bleeding (*Amaranthus*) for the *Fuchsia*.

Spring

Having tubs of contrasting heights and diameters allows you to group them in a classic threesome, two side by side or just one packed with bulbs like this hyacinth and daffodil extravaganza.

PLANTING THE BULBS

'February Gold' ♀ and 'February Silver' daffodils just might bloom in that month in particularly mild parts of the Britain. Even in March or April though they are exceptional varieties – sturdy, very long lasting and not so far removed from the wild species as to lose their character. 'February Silver' is often in short supply so put in an early order to a specialist bulb company as it goes wonderfully well with 'Delft Blue' and 'Prins Hendrik' hyacinths. Both the daffodils and hyacinths should be planted in September or October.

Summer

If you want to give your tubs that smart, co-ordinated look, establish a common link between them. This can be done by repeating a plant or, more subtly, a colour in each one. Red is prevalent in this cluster of pots, a theme set up by the extraordinary starfish-like *Fascicularia* in the foreground echoed in the tub of coneflowers, coleus, *Pelargonium* and busy lizzies. Best of all though was the *Fuchsia* tub, which is isolated here for closer inspection.

STARTING WITH SEED

It takes a little more effort to gather a tender perennial (variegated busy lizzie), a herbaceous perennial (*Houttuynia*), a half-hardy annual (Prince of Wales feathers) and a half-hardy perennial (*Fuchsia* 'Thalia'), but the result is four times more satisfying than a tub of red *Pelargonium*. Sow Prince of Wales feathers in March in a warm greenhouse or on a windowsill. Plant them out in a sunny, sheltered spot in early to mid-June.

Buy the busy lizzies as plug plants but wait until June before shopping for *Houttuynia*. Add in a good-sized *Fuchsia* and the quartet is complete. It may be July before you really see the red coming through, but it keeps on coming until October.

▷ *I draped a grape vine and some empty pots around my red-themed tubs. Behind, grey, purple and yellow foliage flatter the more flamboyant summer performers.*

Autumn

At maple time, in October, sizeable specimens of Japanese varieties thrill me and my visitors right outside the French windows. Beneath this sunset canopy I like to lay on a few more theatrical touches, using ornamental cabbages and kale – appropriately enough as many are bred in Japan – and dwarf chrysanthemums. An oriental style becomes almost inescapable. To extend the daylight hours and viewing opportunities I have arranged spotlights to target the star turns. Imagine drawing back the curtains and being greeted by such a show in your own lounge. It's a lot easier than you might imagine.

FRUITING PARTNERS

Dwarf chrysanths and fancy brassicas really do work well together – pink with pink, white with white, yellow with purple, matching or contrasting colours. In my two wooden tubs I added a third variety: fruiting pernettya in berry colours that fitted neatly into the scheme of things. It's best to treat yourself to sizeable specimens of each. Sit the cabbage and kale rosettes on the tub rim and angle them forward towards your viewpoint. Add the pernettya, snipping off any straggly shoots that may hide the berries. Finally lift up the brassica leaves and fill in the back with your chrysanths.

△ *Among early autumn tints don't forget late-summer flowering plants such as these nasturtiums,* Gaillardia, *French marigolds and* Tagetes, Dahlia, Coreopsis, Lobelia cardinalis *and* Calceolaria.

AUTUMN ILLUMINATIONS

Now what about those maples? Fortunately they settle down very well in containers. My *Acer palmatum* 'Osakazuki' for example has been in a pot for 15 years. Being mobile it also allows me to position it where it will have the maximum impact, and if late spring frosts threaten I move it nearer the house. The cut-leaved varieties are equally impressive, especially in oriental, ceramic bowls. Alongside pink chrysanths and cabbage they are exquisite, even when the leaves fall.

GOOD SUBSTITUTES

For a brighter contrast, use a yellow chrysanth behind purple cabbages and kale.

▷ *Who could wish for a more perfect picture than this:* Chrysanthemum *'Lynn' above pink cabbage and a sprinkling of maple leaves.*

▷ *Special plants deserve a special setting so group your containers together among permanent planting and keep adding new varieties as one goes over.*

Winter

When in winter those fencelines and borders are beginning to look a bit thin why not take comfort from an arrangement of seasonal plants that radiate so much heat and light that you could almost warm your hands on them. Evergreens will be top of the shopping list, but there are also shrubs with coloured stems and twigs to work in. Miss out on them now and you won't get another opportunity. As you will see here, even without the sparkle of early bulbs you can still create a stir and it only takes an hour or so to slot in the pieces and interlock them like a puzzle.

WINTER OPTIONS

Many good garden centres and nurseries will lay on a special, seasonal display of coloured twigs, berries, buds, flowers and foliage. This is just the place to try a few plants associations. Hold one plant against another and see if it pleases the eye. This is my winter playground. Each year I buy a *Skimmia japonica* 'Rubella', a pernettya and some winter heathers. All the rest are grown on in pots from one year to the next – an invaluable resource to dip into, like having all the cake-baking ingredients in the kitchen cupboard.

THREE OR ONE?

Only you can decide if you like to see your plants in splendid isolation as individual specimens, one per tub, or in a more sociable gathering like the interwoven evergreens on the opposite page. If you are a picture maker then you will see the juxtaposition of one plant against another as the element that puts the art into gardening. In the largest tub, position a good-sized *Choisya* at the rear then fill in with the other evergreens, each time threading them though each other so the colours intermingle. Choose at least two varieties that will drape over the rim.

Alternatively pick three contrasting, specimen-sized conifers – pyramidal, round and spreading – to make a classic trio, or use the same tub configuration and add more variety, keeping one tub exclusively for a specimen evergreen. Both approaches work well.

△ *Before you choose your plant selection, it's helpful to surround yourself with the season's finest and mix and match to find the best combinations.*

WINTER RECIPE

JAN	FEB	MAR	APR	MAY	JUN
JUL	AUG	SEP	OCT	NOV	DEC

YOU WILL NEED

- I mature *Skimmia japonica* 'Rubella' ♀ (I)
- I female pernettya (*Gaultheria mucronata* ♀) (2)
- I mature winter heather (*Erica* × *darleyensis*) (3)
- I mature Mexican orange blossom (*Choisya ternata* 'Sundance' ♀) (4)
- I sawara cypress (*Chamaecyparis pisifera* 'Filifera Aurea' ♀) (5)
- broken polystyrene chunks or crocks
- 20 litres ericaceous (lime-free) potting compost

GOOD SUBSTITUTES

In cold areas use *Thuja occidentalis* 'Rheingold' ♀ instead of the *Choisya*.

FOR CONTINUITY

Tuck in some 9cm (3½in) pots of dwarf bulbs among the foliage in February and March.

▷ *Three contrasting, mature conifers will do much to soften a large expanse of bare paving.*

▷▷ *If you introduce more varieties, avoid tiny specimens that will register only close up. Aim to use plants that will make an impact from the house windows.*

◁ *This interwoven selection of coloured buds, leaves, berries and flowers will really light up your winter garden for months in a warm, sheltered spot.*

SPRING RECIPE

JAN FEB MAR APR MAY JUN
JUL AUG SEP OCT NOV DEC

YOU WILL NEED

* 10 early double 'Peach Blossom'
tulips (1)
* 4 'Artemis' pansies (2)
* 1 spurge (*Euphorbia* × *martinii*♥) (3)
* 2 variegated granny's bonnets
(*Aquilegia vulgaris* Vervaeneana Group
'Woodside') (4)
* broken polystyrene chunks or crocks
* 20 litres multipurpose potting
compost

GOOD SUBSTITUTES

Red and yellow 'Fringed Beauty'
tulips look dazzling with yellow
pansies. *Euphorbia amygdaloides*
'Purpurea' has purple leaves.

FOR CONTINUITY

Replace the tulips with two *Dicentra*
'Bacchanal' or 'Pearl Drops'.

Decorated Terracotta Pots

Swags of fruits and flowers are hallmarks of Italian terracotta pots. Some rims are plain, others impressed with a pattern. Faces sometimes peep out among scrolls of foliage. The composition of the clay and lower firing temperatures make them less frost-proof than equivalent British-made ones.

LARGE POT
Height 50cm (20in)
Diameter 46cm (18in)
Weight 25kg (55lb)

SMALL POT
Height 33cm (13in)
Diameter 33cm (13in)
Weight 18kg (40lb)

Spring

There's no doubting the impact one big, impressive pot can have compared to a motley group of smaller ones. You can pack a great deal in using individual plants to form bold blocks or blend them more randomly. Both styles are shown below, with their common links – tulips and a classy spurge.

ROW BY ROW

Don't be timid with tulips and pansies as extrovert as these. Divide the pot into three sections: the front third for a block of pansies; the middle for the tulips; and the back, to act as a foil, for subtle greens and pale yellows.

To achieve this sort of uniformity, pot up the tulips in 13cm (5in) black plastic pots in autumn and move them into your display pot in early March. The first flowers from shop-bought spring pansies are the largest and most impressive and appear conveniently when these early double tulips peak. Autumn-planted pansies will have spread more and produce smaller but more plentiful flowers.

Spurge and granny's bonnets will also be starting to peak so use their fresh foliage as a backdrop. The spurge will still be in bloom when the granny's bonnets flower in May.

TULIP MANIA

Tulips have much better-quality leaves than daffodils. Some have a blue sheen, others such as 'Red Riding Hood'♥ are marked with dark stripes, but best of all are the variegated varieties such as *T. praestans* 'Unicum'. These silver-edged 'Esperanto' (left) look good for weeks, especially among grey leaves and pastel flowers. The green-and-white-feathered tulip flowers also contain flashes of china rose.

I interplanted them with blue and white 'Royal Delft' pansies and edged them with *Hebe pinguifolia* 'Pagei'♥. These two can form the nucleus of a June and July display if you follow the non-stop growplan on the opposite page.

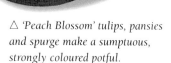

△ *'Peach Blossom' tulips, pansies and spurge make a sumptuous, strongly coloured potful.*

◁ *Here tulips and pansies are used in a more random, tranquil mix.*

Summer

Many keen and knowledgeable gardeners dispute the term 'June gap'. However, when you've pulled up the wallflowers and tulips, are looking longingly at the lilies for buds and the summer bedding is still in its infancy, it's worth considering a few ideas to maintain interest in your containers.

There are now plenty of tempting herbaceous perennials on show, and in June and July herbs are probably at their best with fresh, aromatic foliage in fascinating colours and textures. Some such as chives should also be valued for their flowers.

BACKGROUND PLANNING

If you've got a good patch of self-sown hardy annuals such as poached egg flower, pot marigolds or these love-in-a-mist backed by dense foliage, then why not station your decorated pot where it can rise up majestically from the undergrowth. This approach really flatters the chives and cranesbill, which replaced the tulips and spurge from the spring arrangement.

Regular deadheading and a weekly liquid feed have kept the 'Royal Delft' pansies flowering merrily. Their whiskery faces and blue flashes picked up the cranesbill petals to perfection.

POTTED RHODODENDRONS

To cross the divide between spring and summer consider using dwarf *Rhododendron* whose needs are ideally suited to pot culture. Yakushimanum hybrids are setting the pace. They have tidy foliage and scrumptious flowers that often appear darker before they develop fully.

This 'Yaku Queen' reminds me of vanilla ice-cream dripping with raspberry syrup. Pink- and plum-coloured pansies carry this raspberry ripple theme to the rim of the pot. Variegated *Astrantia* and forget-me-nots make soothing go betweens.

△ *To keep up interest in the pot, the pansies and* Hebe *from the spring tulip container have been retained and enhanced with chives and geranium.*

SUMMER RECIPE

JAN	FEB	MAR	APR	MAY	JUN
JUL	AUG	SEP	OCT	NOV	DEC

YOU WILL NEED
- 2 chives (*Allium schoenoprasum*) (1)
- 1 cranesbill (*Geranium ibericum*) (2)
- 4 'Royal Delft' pansies (3)
- 1 *Hebe pinguifolia* 'Pagei' ♔ (4)
- broken polystyrene chunks or crocks
- 14 litres multipurpose potting compost (less if this container is being carried on from the spring project).

GOOD SUBSTITUTES
Geranium himalayense 'Plenum' is a very refined, double-flowered cranesbill that looks pretty alongside x *Heucherella alba* 'Rosalie'.

FOR CONTINUITY
Replace the chives and cranesbill with pot-grown *Salvia farinacea* 'Strata' or pastel snapdragons (*Antirrhinum* 'Jamaican Mist'). Top up with compost when you replace a spent plant.

▷ *Don't miss out on a treat like this. Use a dwarf* Rhododendron *to set up the colour theme.*

Autumn

Many people with a small garden will want to make every square foot earn its keep so plants that have coloured leaves and flowers (or fruit) will be especially welcome. *Fuchsia* for example includes gems such as the hardy 'Versicolor' with its pink and red leaves flushed creamy white and elegant flowers as well. I used it to cascade over my decorated pot among some startling foliage colours that gave me some of my favourite plant associations of the year.

MARCH SOWING

You can buy all the plants in this autumn gathering in late summer and early autumn with the exception of the castor oil plant. This should be sown indoors above a radiator, in an airing cupboard or in a heated propagator in March. The plant itself and its seeds are both attractive but highly poisonous so grow purple-leaved *Canna* instead if you're concerned about inquisitive toddlers. Grow them on in warmth until mid-June, when they can be stood outside.

Assemble the other plants and arrange them in their display pot in August. By late September as it knits together you'll be congratulating yourself on your foresight.

△ *These trailing* Sedum ewersii *in the foreground pick up the cabbages' pink, young leaves, veins and midribs. Meanwhile the seed-raised* Aster *'Pruhonicer Dwarf Mixed' is an ideal height to bring up the rear.*

Winter

Imagine the pleasure you would get walking up to a main door on a bleak December day to be greeted by a glowing brazier of red buds and yellow leaves, powdered with snow. With such a potful of colour, which can be made even more dramatic by snaking coloured lights through the evergreens, who needs a Christmas tree?

CHRISTMAS CONTRAST

Arrange your pot in a warm and sheltered site. If it is surrounded by evergreens and fruiting shrubs, so much the better. Contrast is the key with a winter arrangement so choose plants that have different shapes, colours and textures.

A semi-prostrate juniper such as 'Grey Owl' is a fine starting point to soften the rim. *Skimmia japonica* 'Rubella' buds provide the embers, yellow tree heather the flames. Fill out the back with taller, coloured evergreens.

△ *Seek out some of the more unusual evergreens to add sophistication to your winter pot.*

◁◁ *Link your technicolor pot with other striking foliage plants like* Hosta *and* Bergenia *in front and a variegated cabbage palm behind, raised up on a pot.*

AUTUMN RECIPE

JAN	FEB	MAR	APR	MAY	JUN
JUL	AUG	SEP	OCT	NOV	DEC

YOU WILL NEED

- 1 *Fuchsia magellanica* 'Versicolor' ♥ (1)
- 3 castor oil plants (*Ricinus communis* 'Carmencita') (2)
- 1 wormwood (*Artemisia ludoviciana* 'Silver Queen' ♥) (3)
- 3 purple-leaved Northern Lights Series ornamental cabbages (4)
- 2 coleus (*Solenostemon* 'Wizard Mixed') (5)
- broken polystyrene chunks or crocks
- 20 litres multipurpose potting compost

ALTERNATIVELY

For another good *Fuchsia* see page 22.

WINTER RECIPE

JAN	FEB	MAR	APR	MAY	JUN
JUL	AUG	SEP	OCT	NOV	DEC

YOU WILL NEED

- 1 grey-leaved juniper (*Juniperus virginiana* 'Grey Owl' ♥) (1)
- 1 male *Skimmia japonica* 'Rubella' ♥ (2)
- 1 yellow-leaved tree heather (*Erica arborea* 'Albert's Gold' ♥) (3)
- 1 variegated *Osmanthus heterophyllus* 'Goshiki' (4)
- 1 dwarf cypress (*Chamaecyparis pisifera* 'Squarrosa Lombarts') (5)
- broken polystyrene chunks or crocks
- 20 litres multipurpose potting compost

Bamboo Trough

Bamboo is tough and resilient, familiar in its role as fences and screens in Japanese gardens. This painted bamboo trough is a good neutral shade and its proportions allow for some impressive, three-row line-ups on window ledges and tables, inside or out.

Height 15cm (6in)
Width 20cm (8in)
Length 53cm (21in)
Weight 1kg (2lb)

Spring

Half barrels and deep terracotta pots can intimidate many of the more petite spring bulbs and bedding plants. Matching your plants to their container is therefore a matter of scale as well as colour and style. A Japanese arrangement would be perfect for this trough, but I settled on a Dutch theme.

DUTCH PAINTINGS

The rich colours and sculptural qualities of the old-fashioned flowers shown on the opposite page reminded me of early Dutch flower paintings. Although these often took months or years to complete, my planting picture was done in 30 minutes flat.

I started in autumn because dwarf, double 'Hollyhock' hyacinths are not

available in spring and there's nothing else like them. Having potted them up in individual 9cm (3½in) pots, I left them under a warm wall to overwinter. When they were just beginning to show colour, I lined them up in the bamboo trough with auriculas and one of those *Viola* with flecked flowers.

▽ For a different effect take your cue from the colour of the trough. 'Imperial Antique Shades' pansies, pastel primroses and Crocus vernus 'Vanguard' make a memorable mix for late March and April.

▷ Full of romance and character, there is a classic quality to this combination of double hyacinths, auriculas and Viola. 'Tom Thumb' wallflowers would also fit in well and add another perfume.

Summer

Some 60 per cent of bedding plant purchases are for container displays, the most popular colour being pink; orange is the least popular, which is a shame. Colour has a very powerful influence on our moods and emotions, and these days I'm drawn more and more to strong colours: purples and blues with vibrant oranges and yellows.

COLOUR THEMING

Trailing snapdragons are a real novelty, though I didn't manage to achieve anything that resembled those catalogue pictures of hanging baskets dripping with an avalanche of snaps. Anyway, as a theme setter, this front-row combination of pink snapdragons, variegated, pink-flowered *Aptenia* and 'Burgundy Glow' bugle gave me just the right amount of overhang and a pleasing confection of colours. You can buy all three in spring.

To complete the planting, any pale *Petunia* will do as long as they're not supervigorous. *P.* Celebrity Series 'Chiffon Morn', which I grew from seed sown in March, is especially delicate. Nip off dead flowers regularly and squeeze any greenfly on the stalks and opening blooms before they get a foothold.

▽ *The whiskered faces and fascinating colour variants of* Viola *'Bambini' soothe the vivid orange blooms.*

△ *Bamboo troughs make ideal windowboxes, which can be positioned side by side on a wide, recessed sill.*

SUMMER MINIATURES

If you like orange flowers and raising seedlings then you'll love this arrangement. *Tagetes* Safari Series 'Safari Tangerine' must be about the brightest orange of any flower, never mind just French marigolds. Don't unleash it in a big blob. Weave it through two-tone *Lobelia erinus* Riviera Series 'Blue Splash' and the tiny form of yellow-leaved feverfew (*Tanacetum parthenium* 'Golden Moss').

▷▷ *Trailing snapdragons are likely to become immensely popular. Here they toned in beautifully with bugle, soft pink* Petunia *and variegated* Aptenia.

AUTUMN RECIPE

| JAN | FEB | MAR | APR | MAY | JUN |
| JUL | AUG | **SEP** | **OCT** | **NOV** | DEC |

YOU WILL NEED

- 2 dwarf, pink chrysanths (*Chrysanthemum* 'Lynn') (1)
- 3 autumn crocuses (*Colchicum* 'Waterlily') (2)
- 3 white and pink busy lizzies from *Impatiens* 'Pantomime Mixed' (3)
- plastic liner
- broken polystyrene chunks or crocks
- 10 litres multipurpose potting compost

GOOD SUBSTITUTES

Try *Colchicum speciosum* ♥ instead of 'Waterlily', which is rather expensive and in short supply, being one of the most desirable of all double flowers.

FOR CONTINUITY

Plant out the *Colchicum* and chrysanths together in a sunny border and add michaelmas daisies and dwarf Japanese anemones to build up the picture.

ALTERNATIVELY

See *Colchicum* in a completely different setting on page 80.

Autumn

If you garden in a very traditional fashion with one eye constantly on the text book and the other on the calendar, then you'll be missing out on a lot of the excitement and fun of this hobby. In the future, I'm convinced that more and more of our living garden components will arrive through the post, especially the ephemeral ones like bedding plants. Bulbs remain popular mail-order items and if you want something a little rare or different your best bet is to order that by post, too. This autumn recipe all arrived by post, some plants with rather better timing than others.

ADVANCE PLANNING

There's no reason why you can't buy your chrysanths in September as fully grown plants on the point of flower. On sale you'll also find huge, dry bulbs of pink autumn crocus in varieties like 'Lilac Wonder'. Add your own (or a gardening friend's) busy lizzies and you have the start of a subtle scheme for a trough like this or a windowbox or shallow bowl.

I arrived by a different route. I bought the busy lizzies and dwarf chrysanths as plug plants. They arrived in April and were potted up and grown on

△ *With the help of a little sunlight these* Colchicum *soon recovered from their postal journey and turned from anaemic white to pink.*

until I needed them. I ordered the exquisite 'Waterlily' autumn crocus bulbs from a specialist grower and within minutes had them installed among all these soft, sensuous pinks. Could anything be more convenient or satisfying?

TIME TO RECOVER

Colchicum has sufficient reserves in its bulbs to be able to flower freely without food or water. This was just as well, because mine were gasping when I unwrapped them.

◁ *Give summer busy lizzies a new lease of life by matching their colours to autumn chrysanths. Bring the trough indoors if frost is forecast.*

△ *The* Colchicum *'Waterlily' flower stalks are shorter than more robust varieties such as 'Lilac Wonder', so work the bulbs into the front half of the trough.*

Winter

Most properties will have a cool porch, conservatory, veranda or greenhouse that escapes the worst of the rain and frost, and these are the perfect settings for my scented container filled with forced hyacinths and florists' primroses. A lightweight bamboo trough such as this can always go out on fine days and be bought indoors if the weather turns particularly cold or wet. The heady perfume from so many hyacinths however may be overpowering in a small room.

ROOT GROWTH

If you decide to force your own hyacinth bulbs remember that success or failure depends on the development of an adequate root system before they are brought into the warmth. Prepared bulbs can be bought and planted from mid-September for Christmas flowering. Pot them in individual 9cm (3½in) pots and leave them in a cold, dark place – the base of the north-facing wall is ideal. When the flower buds are 6–7.5cm (2½–3in) long, bring the plants indoors to force on.

SCENT FOR WINTER

Though not quite as universal as pot chrysanths, professional growers sow primroses from April to July for sale in autumn, winter and spring, and there are some stunning varieties. Choose a range of colours that will tone in with forced hyacinths such as these 'Anna Marie'.

△ *Position your trough on a table in a central area indoors and let the hyacinths fill the whole house with their penetrating perfume.*

WINTER RECIPE

JAN	FEB	MAR	APR	MAY	JUN
JUL	AUG	SEP	OCT	NOV	DEC

YOU WILL NEED
- 10 treated hyacinth bulbs for forcing (*Hyacinthus orientalis* 'Anna Marie'♀) (1)
- 5 florists' primroses (*Primula* Charisma Series) (2)
- plastic liner
- broken polystyrene chunks or crocks
- 10 litres multipurpose potting compost

GOOD SUBSTITUTES
Pick out your favourite hyacinth colours, then choose primroses that will harmonise or contrast with them.

FOR CONTINUITY
To keep the primroses company, replace the hyacinths with forced daffodils such as 'Tête-à-Tête'. Hyacinths produce smaller spikes after forcing but it is still worth planting the spent bulbs in a border.

ALTERNATIVELY
For another unique pairing that features pink primroses see page 82.

◁ *As your primroses start to go over, why not reserve a semi-shady bed in the garden where you can plant them out. Enrich the bed with garden compost or composted bark and add polyanthus and dwarf spring bulbs too. Don't let slugs enjoy them more than you.*

YOU WILL NEED

- 5 wallflowers (*Erysimum cheiri* Bedder Series 'Orange Bedder') (1)
- 10 early, single 'Generaal de Wet' tulips (2)
- 3 or 4 golden-leaved feverfew (*Tanacetum parthenium* 'Aureum') (3)
- 4 'Padparadja' pansies (4)
- 10 'Modern Art' daffodils (5)
- broken polystyrene chunks or crumpled compost bags to pack out the bottom half of the water tank
- 30 litres multipurpose potting compost

FOR CONTINUITY

Retain the pansy and feverfew edge and fill in behind with orange African marigolds (*Tagetes*) and yellow, trailing *Bidens* 'Golden Eye'.

ALTERNATIVELY

To see the same tulip among a much more free and easy range of colours turn to page 119.

Victorian Watercart

Chariot-like watercarts could become the most convenient way to store and distribute water, should climate changes make it necessary to decant bath water for use in the garden. It was not just nostalgia that drove me to buy this watercart at a local auction. Such carts really are useful not only as planters but also generally in the garden.

Height 50cm (20in)
Width 40 cm (16in)
Length 53 cm (21in)
Weight 30kg (66lb)

Spring

What a luxury to have a container that you can put almost anywhere in the garden, but never actually lift. This consideration makes the choice of background almost as important as what's in the planter itself. In spring, daffodils in grass or orchard blossom would be an irresistible link to a yellow-and-white or pink-and-white, colour-themed display in the cart. I chose a delicious mix of orange and yellow that would look great in any sizeable container.

CITRUS SCHEMES

To add zest to your containers, introduce themed spring displays around citrus fruits: lemon and lime; orange and lemon. You might almost think of a bowl of fruit when you look at a modern daffodil with those outrageous, frilly, orange centres. If you like the idea of an orange and lemon theme, you'll need to start planning almost a year in advance, because you usually find only mixed bunches of wallflowers for sale in late summer.

Sow wallflower seed in June, pinch them out when they're a few inches tall, and transplant them to sever the tap root to encourage big, bushy plants.

▷ *In early April, plant the bulbs in position and finish off with orange pansies and golden-leaved feverfew along the front edge. When the sun shines it will be the brightest spot in the garden.*

Alternatively, pot up two bundles of mixed colours in September, wait till they show flower colour and pick out the yellows and oranges.

POTTING UP BULBS

Pot up the tulips and daffodils three or four to a 15cm (6in) pot, so you can plant them out in bud with pinpoint accuracy. Daffodils are more prone to drying out than tulip bulbs so the earlier the better for those, September being ideal. Tulips can wait until November with no ill effects.

◁ *The coppery red, new growth on Photinia × fraseri 'Red Robin' ♀ provides a wonderful backdrop for oranges and yellows. Even if you haven't got a watercart to elevate your container you can always site an urn nearby or raise a large pot on bricks.*

▷ *Be daring with your spring bedding and restrict the colours to yellow and orange. The result looks good enough to eat and the wallflowers and tulips both have a sweet scent too.*

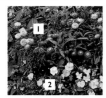
△ *To prevent seed capsules forming, check pansies every few days and remove any blooms as soon as the petals start to curl.*

Summer

Many planting ideas rely on restricting the rainbow of colours to achieve their impact. At times however it's good to let rip with mixtures, especially when they're varieties such as pansies and strawflowers that have plenty of poise and character. They could just be the plants to tempt children to take an interest in container gardening themselves. Plant up a really big patch of each, so you get the full spectrum of colours.

SOWING AND GROWING

These 'Bright Bikini Mixed' strawflowers are purely for garden decoration, though there's no reason why a keen flower arranger can't line out some extra plants in a couple of rows on some spare ground to cut and dry for a winter arrangement. This eight-colour mixture reaches 38cm (15in) high and is far better for display work than taller, lanky types. They're also great fun with *Viola* such as 'Monarch Mixed'.

Sow the strawflowers and *Viola* in March under glass or indoors and grow them on – three plants to a 15cm (6in) pot – until they are just about to flower. Then move them to your display container to see out the summer.

△ *Plant your pot-grown strawflowers in the back two-thirds of the container before adding the* Viola.

STRAWBERRY SURPRISE

For something different to peak in August and September try this appetising mixture of 'Strawberry Parfait' pinks, purple-leaved ornamental kale, multicoloured, trailing *Lobelia* and the unusual annual *Matricaria* 'Santana Lemon'. You'll have to sow seeds of the *Matricaria* in March or April, but it's worth the trouble.

'Strawberry Parfait' is one of a range of chinensis pinks grown by nurserymen to pep up flagging containers in summer. This colour blend is hard to resist; if you want a lot, sow your own seed.

◁ *Although it's a bit more work to achieve, this attractive blend of foliage and flower colour is rich and rewarding.*

▷ *These dainty* Viola *are better at masking the front edge of a container than larger-flowered pansies and they look particularly good with the strawflowers.*

Autumn

Sometimes a gardener is caught out by drought, pests and diseases, an overvigorous plant or, conversely, one that fails to fill its allocated space. As a result an unsightly gap may occur in the border. One quick way to plug the gap is with an autumn container brimming with some of the season's finest offerings. When you see how uplifting it can be, you might rally more recruits to build up a real hot spot in the border. Don't worry if you haven't got a watercart; a planted wheelbarrow will fill a bare patch just as well.

△ Chrysanths bought as young rooted cuttings in late spring and early summer will begin to peak by September and continue to bloom well into autumn.

EXPAND THE THEME

Look around your border for a key plant to set up the colour theme. It could be a pink cabbage or *Dahlia*, yellow coneflowers, blue *Hydrangea* or *Aster* or another foliage plant. Then link in with that. Dwarf chrysanths or michaelmas daisies can be relied upon to give you the bones of your container.

I bought two ice plants to sit under my pink chrysanths and, to soften the edges, blue fescue grass. Trailing forms of knotgrass with their red and brown, burnished leaves make an excellent choice to cascade over the rim. To finish off, hide a few fat autumn crocus bulbs among the foliage in the front half of the container. Like magic they will nose through and burst out to rapturous applause.

AUTUMN RECIPE

JAN	FEB	MAR	APR	MAY	JUN
JUL	AUG	SEP	OCT	NOV	DEC

YOU WILL NEED

- 2 dwarf chrysanths (*Chrysanthemum* 'Lynn') (1)
- 2 ice plants (*Sedum spectabile* 'Brilliant' ♀) (2)
- 2 blue fescue grass (*Festuca glauca* 'Elijah Blue') (3)
- 1 knotgrass (*Persicaria affinis* 'Donald Lowndes' ♀) (4)
- 4 autumn crocus (*Colchicum* 'Lilac Wonder') (5)
- broken polystyrene chunks or crumpled compost bags to pack out the bottom half of the water tank
- 30 litres multipurpose potting compost

Winter

To avoid a conifer that grows into a monster, a good rule of thumb is to choose one that is small and expensive as it's most probably a dwarf. If it's five times the size and half the price, it's probably a hedging variety. Some of the best conifers, such as this prostrate blue fir, will always be expensive as they reflect the expertise needed to grow them.

PRIZED FIR

This top-of-the-range, blue-needled conifer with its low, swooping habit could have been made for my watercart. I wheeled the cart up under the house windows in November and gave my fir pride of place at the front. I backed it with blue and black pansies and *Houttuynia*. The *Houttuynia* however will need replacing with a yellow, dwarf conifer after the first hard frost.

▷ Extra plants positioned around the base of your container add interest and help to 'root' it to the spot.

◁ My watercart became an irresistible focal point in a sea of coloured winter foliage.

WINTER RECIPE

JAN	FEB	MAR	APR	MAY	JUN
JUL	AUG	SEP	OCT	NOV	DEC

YOU WILL NEED

- 1 mature, prostrate blue fir (*Abies procera* 'Glauca Prostrata') (1)
- 5 blue and black Universal Series ♀ pansies (2)
- 1 *Houttuynia cordata* 'Chameleon' (3)
- broken polystyrene chunks or crumpled compost bags to pack out the bottom half of the water tank
- 30 litres multipurpose potting compost

Blue-glazed Pot

These heavy, glazed pots are virtually impervious to the elements – contrary to what is often said about the frost hardiness of glazed containers. Imported from China, they have boosted the popularity of container gardening and created exciting opportunities for colour-themed displays. This hexagonal pot – a feature in itself – looks good with flowers and foliage tumbling over the rim.

Spring

To me, bright blue plastic containers are as useful as weathered stone or terracotta ones and a common plant with desirable qualities gives me just as much pleasure as a rarity. It all depends on what you can do with the pots and plants – their potential for picture-making. I much prefer a common rock rose to a spring alpine that has to spend half its life under a sheet of glass to keep off winter wet. In this spring planting I have however introduced a rarity that has impeccable credentials as a container plant and is destined to make a real impact on our gardens.

Height 33cm (13in)
Diameter 33cm (13in)
Weight 20kg (44lb)

EAST MEETS WEST

Corydalis flexuosa in the wild grows on steep, shady slopes in western Sichuan in China and follows the same pattern of summer dormancy as it does when cultivated in this country, so don't worry if it disappears in July. This gem has purple-spotted leaves. When planted with pink hybrid primroses you are contrasting one plant created after years of intensive breeding with another one straight from the wild.

COLOUR SCHEMING

The idea of a single-colour theme for a container presents an interesting challenge though don't become a slave to the colour of your choice – in this case yellow. Black-faced, purple-winged, yellow pansies will add a magical touch. This predominantly yellow nest (left) also contains purple-leaved spurge, yellow-leaved creeping Jenny and meadowsweet and variegated *Hosta* 'Ground Master'.

▽ *Site this pot in semi-shade to prevent newly emerged, tender leaves from scorching in the spring sun.*

Summer

One of my most useful gardening experiences was working in the plant advice office of a large garden centre. I was often asked to name a plant that provided colour for 365 days a year. Customers wanted a single plant that would provide flowers, berries, autumn colour, bright stems and evergreen foliage; perfume would be nice too and of course it must be able to grow absolutely anywhere. We used to recommend *Cotoneaster lacteus*♀ as it had four of these qualities.

A couple of years ago I discovered a new shrub – *Hypericum androsaemum* 'Gladys Brabazon' – that has an impressive track record. It boasts irregular, white-and-pink variegation and yellow flowers followed by red berries that turn black as they age and persist into winter. Here's how I displayed this form of our native tutsan.

BUILD A FRAME

It may be a bit unconventional, but there are a range of spreading shrubs for summer containers that can be planted in the middle of your pot and surrounded by bedding threaded through their flowering or fruiting branches. As well as tutsan, other suitable shrubs are sun rose (*Cistus*), *Hebe*, shrubby *Potentilla* and carpeting roses.

I bought five pot-grown floss flowers in July to make a cool, lavender-blue pool through the tutsan stems. They fitted in all the gaps and took the bareness off the shrub.

For the backdrop I used a pot-grown 'Little Joy' lily whose striped petals picked up the tutsan berries to perfection and which would enjoy having its roots in shade behind the blue-glazed pot. Have at least a dozen dwarf lilies as backups so that you can make the same last-minute scene changes when necessary. A spiky-leaved grass and grey and white *Anaphalis* completed the stage scenery. You can keep this colourful bank going until the frosts by changing the backdrop plants around regularly. Perhaps this is the solution to that year-round, non-stop colour parade – the gardener's Holy Grail.

▷ *With the berry pot in position, build up a backdrop of planting so it merges seamlessly into a bank of foliage and flower.*

◁ *These gentle* Corydalis *colours tone in beautifully with the blue-glazed pot.*

▽ *Although unusual, a large fruiting shrub can be successfully surrounded by smaller pot-grown bedding plants.*

Autumn

I'm as susceptible to new arrivals on the plant scene as any other keen gardener, even though some novelties fail to stand the test of time. The future however is bright for bud heathers, which excel during the gap between the late-summer flowering kinds and the winter varieties. I was

pleased with these, especially as the colours toned in so well with two variegated evergreens and two ragged, purple-leaved 'Red Peacock' kale plants that I had earmarked for my blue-glazed pot. I wove them all together to create a glorious carpet as intense in colour as any summer showpiece. Here's how to make your peacock parade.

ORNAMENTAL FOLIAGE

Start off by positioning two good-sized, purple or pink ornamental cabbages or kale in the centre of your pot. Angle the rosettes slightly away from each other. Fill in behind with two variegated *Hebe*; in cold areas, substitute a variegated *Euonymus* for the less hardy *Hebe*. Thread the *Leucothoe* through the kale leaves and finally drift the bud heathers along the rim and back into the kale.

◁ *Sit back and enjoy this autumnal feast of purple, green and white planted in the soft grey-blue, glazed pot.*

Winter

Despite sharp-eyed blackbirds, the fruits on show here are quite capable of lasting a full six months or more especially if you grow them in a container by a busy thoroughfare near the house. Don't expect the same sort of life-span from pyracantha berries, as they are the most sought-after fruits by hungry birds.

COLOURFUL BERRIES

Look out for three contrasting berry colours for your collection. Laurustinus berries are an amazing blue colour, frequently tucked away inside the foliage so don't be afraid to snip off a few shoots to reveal them. Only larger, specimen-sized plants will have fruits and flower buds together. Yellow, grassy-leaved *Acorus* will add a bit of sparkle and provide a brilliant contrast to the red *Skimmia* fruits.

▷ *One big, bold, berrying evergreen will form the backbone in this blue-glazed pot in winter. Then allow the Skimmia, Acorus and Gaultheria to run into each other at the front.*

▷ *Who needs flowers when you can generate this intensity of colour with berries and coloured foliage? Repeat the yellow Acorus in a pot below.*

Basketwork Pot and Pans

Hand-thrown pots and pans with strapwork decoration and gracefully curving sides are among the most popu~~lar~~ and elegant of all designs. Most carry a guarantee against surface flaking by frost and will give years of pleasure, though the handles are comparatively fragile.

Spring

Although spring bulbs look undeniably good in a pair of these flared, round pans, when placed side by side such identical containers lack style. Raise one and put the other further forward on feet and the scene is transformed. Daffodils such as 'Lemon Beauty' that nod their heads, shy to reveal their crowning glory, also benefit from a bit of height so their scented blooms are nearer passers-by.

To link pots you can use colour or repeat a plant. At flowering time, partner 'Lemon Beauty' with the early, stocky 'Purissima' tulips for colour and height. Their yellow centres are fully revealed only in bright sunlight. Underplant with white, double daisies and *Arabis* in autumn or spring. A dressing of coarse gravel will stop mud splashing and help to support the bulb stems a little.

ROUND PAN	PAN WITH HANDLES	POT
Height	Height	Height
23cm (9in)	14cm (5½in)	38cm (15in)
Diameter	Width	Diameter
35cm (14in)	25cm (10in)	43cm (17in)
Weight	Length	Weight
9kg (20lb)	30cm (12in)	22kg (48lb)
	Weight	
	5kg (11lb)	

△ *Pot up your bulbs into 15cm (6in) plastic pots in autumn. Transfer them to their display pots in late March, pulling out any stunted or failed flowers so that each panful is perfect.*

◁ *Look out for daffodil and tulip varieties that have similar heights, colours and flowering times and feature them in matching pans.*

Summer

Cottage pinks, with their evocative, clove-like scent and blowsy buttons, are an essential ingredient of any richly romantic jumble of summer flowers. They do require sun and good drainage but if you garden on waterlogged clay you can still enjoy them in pots. Why not assemble a collection, each variety in an individual pot, or you could mix them – the complementary planting giving their wiry stems something to lean on.

FRAGRANT DISPLAY

Raised as recently as 1980, this deep red 'Houndspool Cheryl' is a relatively modern variety of pink yet still full of character. To throw the flowers into sharp focus and build on the scented theme, why not work in a background of aromatic, variegated leaves. *Origanum vulgare* 'County Cream' is a must for herb addicts, well worth seeking out from specialist suppliers or large garden centres.

△ To make a real impact with pinks, you'll need larger plants than those generally available in 9cm (3¹/₂in) pots. These were bought as young plugs the previous spring and grown on for a year.

▽ Pinks are highly sociable plants, so be bold and mix them in with other summer favourites.

SUMMER RECIPE

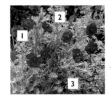

JAN	FEB	MAR	APR	MAY	JUN
JUL	AUG	SEP	OCT	NOV	DEC

YOU WILL NEED

- 5 mature pinks (*Dianthus* 'Houndspool Cheryl' ♀) (1)
- 3 variegated oregano (*Origanum vulgare* 'County Cream') (2)
- 2 rock daisies (*Brachyscome multifida*) (3)
- broken polystyrene chunks or crocks
- 30 litres multipurpose potting compost

GOOD SUBSTITUTES

Try *Tagetes* Gem Series 'Lemon Gem' instead of, or as well as, the variegated oregano. For two-tone, red flowers, *Dianthus* 'Laced Monarch' is a delight.

FOR CONTINUITY

By late July, the pinks will be spent so plant them out in a border beneath roses and *Campanula* and fill in with a scented *Petunia* such as Mirage Series 'Mirage Lavender'.

▷ Expand the fragrant theme and plant up the handled pan with three of your favourite thymes. Select one or two with yellow or variegated leaves and don't forget to contrast the flower colours too – all very drought resistant and highly tactile!

Autumn

Much has been made of the seemingly unrelenting rise in world temperatures and reduction in rainfall, which is worrying for us gardeners. Container gardening however can be a very water-effective way to enjoy plants because every drop goes directly to the plants' roots. If the plants themselves are also able to survive a spell without water, you needn't feel guilty about having a short holiday. All plants in my autumn pot are drought resistant and look good too.

DROUGHT-TOLERANT PLANTS

Fleshy, succulent leaves and stems are a reliable sign that plants such as stonecrops tolerate dry conditions. Grasses such as these fescues also have a classic adaptation to drought: their leaves are rolled to conceal the pores through which water is lost. To increase moisture retention in a planter, add water-retaining granules to the compost and topdress the surface with a thick layer of gravel.

I picked out two contrasting *Sedum*, putting 'Herbstfreude' at the back of the pot as it's the biggest and boldest, then two shorter plants below and edged up with the grasses.

△ *To enjoy the stonecrop seedheads as they bleach and skeletonise, do not deadhead after flowering. The dwarf grasses also look ghostly in winter sprinkled with frost.*

▷ *Combine fleshy- and grassy-leaved plants that not only look good all summer but also produce flowers in late summer and autumn.*

Winter

To create maximum impact from a limited area of garden, underplant bulbs with groundcover. This, in effect, doubles your colour. In the wild, bluebells grow up through wood anemones, and who would settle for a plain carpet of winter heathers when the alternative is to pepper them with jewel-like spring bulbs. It works in pots as well as beds.

MATCHMAKING

Avoid tall, leafy bulbs such as hyacinths and daffodils and tulips over about 23cm (9in) tall. *Crocus* with its wispy leaves and precocious flowers is ideal to plant with low-growing winter heathers. You can pot them up in autumn and transfer them to your pan on the point of flower as I've done here or plant the bulbs and heathers directly into the display pot in autumn. There is no finer *Crocus* than this tricoloured gem, open or closed. A dressing of fine grit prevents compost washing down the sides.

▷ *Choose only low-growing winter heathers if you want your Crocus flowers to emerge from among their wiry stems.*

Three-way Trough

With just a few basic carpentry skills, it's easy to make your own unique windowboxes and troughs. This three-way trough has a removable plinth and an add-on roof that turns it into an alpine chalet. Line your box with plastic or build it around a rigid plastic trough to keep damp potting compost and timber apart.

Height 23cm (9in)
Width 23cm (9in)
Length 60cm (24in)
Weight 6kg (13lb)

SPRING RECIPE

JAN	FEB	MAR	APR	MAY	JUN
JUL	AUG	SEP	OCT	NOV	DEC

YOU WILL NEED

- 20 *Narcissus* 'Jetfire' (1)
- 5 blue-and-white Turbo Series pansies (2)
- plastic liner
- broken polystyrene chunks or crocks
- 16 litres multipurpose potting compost

GOOD SUBSTITUTES

For a more pastel colour scheme try cream-and-lemon *Narcissus* 'Topolino' with 'Imperial Pink Shades' pansies.

ALTERNATIVELY

Narcissus 'Jetfire' has new partners on page 105.

Spring

'Jetfire' daffodils are tailor-made for windowboxes and troughs. These precocious, sturdy, large-flowered, dwarf bulbs have enough of the wild species' long, narrow snout and swept-back petals to betray their affinity with *Narcissus cyclamineus*♀.

There are plenty of good pansies about in April to pair with these daffodils. Choose a clear yellow or orange pansy (or both) to complement the daffodils or contrast them against a selection of blues. Plant up this arrangement in autumn or – as I've done here – in spring.

▷ *For spring planting, pot up the 'Jetfire' bulbs in autumn and transplant them into the trough in March, once you have bought the pansies.*

Summer

There's no doubt that the New Guinea busy lizzies are more refined and exotic than their smaller-flowered, more familiar counterparts. An increasing number of flower and leaf colours can be grown from seed, but the most spectacular bicolours and those with the darkest leaves and flashiest variegations must be bought as rooted plants with cultivar names.

SUCCESSFUL PAIRING

Begonia makes a particularly good partner for busy lizzies as it has an equally extrovert nature and the ability to thrive in sun or shade. It is just as intolerant of frost and cold so don't put it outdoors until early to mid-June.

Begonia started from dry corms on a windowsill above a radiator or in a heated propagator will be in flower by July. Line up the *Begonia* at the back of the trough so that the New Guinea busy lizzies will help to support them, though you may need to put in a few twiggy sticks for heavy-weight blooms.

▷ *As they age, the trumpets on Narcissus 'Jetfire' turn a deep orange colour in spring.*

SUMMER RECIPE

JAN	FEB	MAR	APR	MAY	JUN
JUL	AUG	SEP	OCT	NOV	DEC

YOU WILL NEED

- 5 mixed-coloured New Guinea busy lizzies (*Impatiens* New Guinea Group) (1)
- 4 mixed-coloured *Begonia* Crispa Marginata (2)
- plastic liner
- broken polystyrene chunks or crocks
- 16 litres multipurpose potting compost

ALTERNATIVELY

Begonia Crispa Marginata is wheeled out again on page 106.

AUTUMN RECIPE

JAN	FEB	MAR	APR	MAY	JUN
JUL	AUG	SEP	OCT	NOV	DEC

YOU WILL NEED

- 1 *Pelargonium* 'Stadt Bern' (1)
- 1 variegated *Pelargonium* (*P. crispum* 'Variegatum'♀) (2)
- 1 *P.* 'Mr Henry Cox'♀ (3)
- 1 *P.* 'Princess Alexandra' (4)
- 3 coleus (*Solenostemon*) with mixed leaf colours (5)
- 1 *Tradescantia fluminensis* 'Albovittata' (6)
- 1 *Tradescantia zebrina* 'Purpusii'♀ (syn. *Zebrina purpusii*) (7)
- plastic liner
- broken polystyrene chunks or crocks
- 16 litres multipurpose potting compost

GOOD SUBSTITUTES

Variegated *Lysimachia congestiflora* 'Outback Sunset' would make a striking trailer at the front – and has yellow flowers too. Blood leaf (*Iresine lindenii*♀) boasts unique, red-and-pink leaves and, like *Tradescantia*, is a house plant that will enjoy a summer holiday in the garden.

FOR CONTINUITY

Bring the whole trough indoors and overwinter it in a well-lit spot. In spring tidy up and repot the old plants or propagate from their strongest shoots.

Autumn

For entertainment into autumn try this eclectic mix of coloured-leaved *Pelargonium* as the mainstay with coleus and trailing *Tradescantia* filling out the front. Many of the best *Pelargonium* grown for their foliage give a passable show of flowers too, though if you want something more prolific, try one of the green-leaved, dwarf zonal types with those dark horseshoe-shaped markings on each leaf.

ALPINE SCENERY

With the appearance of this bolt-on chalet facade, you might expect to see those prolific Swiss cascade *Pelargonium* on show. This is fine where there is plenty of room below the trough, but they are far too vigorous for a ground-level display.

When choosing *Pelargonium*, remember that some variegated types such as 'Lady Plymouth'♀ and 'Happy Thought'♀ can fill the box by themselves in a season. A scented-leaved variety such as the upright *P. crispum* 'Variegatum' would be welcome in almost any such gathering. Fill in the odd gap with young rooted plants. This 'Mr Henry Cox' was grown from a cutting struck in July.

Coleus can be grown from seed or raised from cuttings. A mature plant overwintered on a warm, sunny windowsill indoors will make a good stock plant from which to propagate in spring. Named varieties bought as young plants will have dramatic leaf colours and often deeply cut leaves. You can buy them by mail order or at early summer gardening shows.

Tradescantia grows surprisingly well outdoors though it is advisable to root some cuttings before the first frost is expected to ensure a supply for the following year.

▷ *Include any suitably sized plants that have good leaves for this late summer and autumn swansong.*

◁ *The foliage alone of variegated* Pelargonium *and coleus creates an eye-catching duo.*

WINTER RECIPE

JAN	FEB	MAR	APR	MAY	JUN
JUL	AUG	SEP	OCT	NOV	DEC

YOU WILL NEED

- 1 mature *Erica carnea* 'R.B. Cooke'🏆 (1)
- 1 mature *Erica* x *darleyensis* 'Jack H. Brummage' (2)
- 1 mature *Erica carnea* 'Pink Spangles'🏆 (3)
- 30 sprigs of evergreen and grey foliage plants and berries (4)

These are: *Cotoneaster horizontalis*🏆, *Elaeagnus* x *ebbingei* 'Limelight', *Euonymus fortunei* 'Golden Prince', *Hebe albicans*🏆, *H.* 'Red Edge'🏆, *Helichrysum italicum* subsp. *serotinum*, silver-variegated *Ilex*

- plastic liner
- broken polystyrene chunks or crocks
- 16 litres multipurpose potting compost

FOR CONTINUITY

Top up with fresh trimmings to replace those that have lost their shine. If you have concealed some beakers in the compost, include a few precocious bulb flowers too. They will be all the more welcome at eye level.

Winter

At the time winter heathers are in full bloom – in late January and February – it may be a struggle to track down suitable partners to fill out the back of your trough. Fortunately an unconventional solution to the problem may lie on your doorstep, because most gardens can produce enough evergreen trimmings and berries to make a lively 'hedge' along the back of your container display.

Just because such trimmings have no roots does not mean that they will last only a day or two. When pushed into damp potting compost, sprigs such as these will stay fresh for weeks in the rarified winter air. Alternatively you could sink some beakers into the compost, add water and fill them with small winter posies.

WINTER HEDGING

Start off with three really big potfuls of winter heather to form the drape along the front. To make a change I picked out a yellow-leaved variety, as winter heathers produce flowers in only the restricted colour range of pinks, reds, purples and white. I bought these in autumn, and made sure they bore plenty of pointed, unopened flower buds.

When planting, space out the heathers and push their rootballs hard up against the inside front panel of the trough, filling in the gaps with potting compost. Then insert a selection of evergreen trimmings, including some grey and silver foliage to act as a foil to the reds and to lend a stark, frosty quality. To warm things up a little add yellow evergreens such as *Elaeagnus* and *Euonymus*.

◁ *Large plants create much more impact than smaller ones would.*

▷ *Firm the compost and push in the cut sprigs along the back.*

YOU WILL NEED

- 10 red, Greigii Group tulips (*Tulipa* 'Red Riding Hood'♡) (1)
- 10 yellow, early double tulips (*T.* 'Monte Carlo'♡) (2)
- 6 forget-me-nots (*Myosotis*) (3)
- 2 granny's bonnets (*Aquilegia vulgaris* Vervaeneana Group 'Woodside') (4)
- 1 variegated *Euonymus* 'Blondy' (5)
- 1 *Spiraea japonica* 'Goldflame'♡ (6)
- broken polystyrene chunks or crocks
- 60 litres multipurpose potting compost

GOOD SUBSTITUTES

For something different, try two varieties of viridiflora tulips that have really amazing streaks of green, yellow and white in their petals: 'Humming Bird' and 'Spring Green'♡.

Giant Plain Terracotta Pot

My smallest container is a Victorian thumb pot for rooting cuttings. At 4cm (1½in) diameter you would hardly notice it alongside this monster, which is 55cm (22in) in diameter. It's one of a pair of Italian imports now 12 years old and not once damaged by frost. I like to position my giant pot in dry parts of the garden among established shrubs and I pack it with flowers and foliage that wouldn't survive at soil level.

Height 50cm (20in)
Diameter 55cm (22in)
Weight 45kg (99lb)

Spring

You could cram 100 tulip bulbs into a pot of these proportions, but on their own they'd look a little overwhelming – as well as stiff and regimented. I gave these red and yellow, April-flowering bulbs a far more romantic, country-cottage flavour by drifting through forget-me-nots and granny's bonnets above a lower storey of coloured leaves.

COLOUR THEMING

'Red Riding Hood' is to tulips what 'Tête-à-Tête' is to the daffodil world: robust, long-flowering and readily available as bulbs in autumn or pot-grown plants in spring. The striped leaves are fascinating and, if raised up in a pot, they won't end up being eaten by slugs. All that riotous red requires watering down a little so thread them through variegated *Euonymus* and granny's bonnets. Pot up a really rich yellow tulip in autumn so that you can place them with precision into the giant plain display pot in early April.

Plant the *Spiraea*, then the yellow tulips. Hem them in with the rest of the foliage plants, leaving the front third of the pot for 'Red Riding Hood' tulips. Lastly drift in some self-sown forget-me-nots dug from a border.

A CHANGE OF EMPHASIS

For a more subtle colour scheme, marry up the hyperactive perennial wallflower *Erysimum* 'Bowles' Mauve'♡ with 'Purissima' tulips and encircle them with grape hyacinths, double daisies and *Aubrieta*. Pick up the colours in the display pot with a carefully chosen background.

▷ *'Purissima' tulips rise up through 'Bowles' Mauve'♡ wallflower and a pretty edging of spring flowers in another action-packed planting idea in the giant terracotta pot.*

△ *The great variety of yellow foliage available for spring pots ranges from copper-tinted* Spiraea *to yellow-variegated* Euonymus *and marbled-leaved granny's bonnets.*

▷ *Clashing tulips are given an air of sophistication by including yellow foliage and a haze of self-sown forget-me-nots.*

▷ *Conjure up your own oasis of foliage and fill in around the base of the pot with smaller varieties to create a great wall of jostling, juicy leaves.*

Summer

Sweet Williams are one of the most underrated of all garden plants and I think I know why. Flowering as they do in June and July, they can be a nuisance if they occupy a space set aside for summer bedding. I overcame this by reserving a sizeable container for them on the patio and mixing in other cottage-garden favourites such as Canterbury bells and cornflowers. This planting produced a crescendo of colour well in advance of all those *Petunia* and African marigolds.

HARDY BEDDING PLANTS

Most gardeners are so immersed in setting up their summer containers in May and early June that they overlook the advantages of using hardy annuals sown the previous autumn.

In autumn, conditions are ideal for sowing hardy annuals such as love-in-a-mist, pot marigolds and cornflowers and planting more unusual biennials such as Canterbury bells and sweet Williams. While you're at it, sow and plant a few extra for lifting in spring and transferring to your containers to peak in early summer.

Bank up the planting with tall Sweet Williams at the back and dwarf cornflowers at the front and position those spectacular Canterbury bells so they swing through a haze of bloom.

COOL CONTRASTS FOR SHADE

A gathering of architectural foliage plants such as *Hosta*, ferns and *Rodgersia* can be bold, sculptural and, on a hot day, cool and refreshing. The *Hosta* will also provide flowers later in summer. 'Frances Williams'♈ is rarely outshone by other varieties of *Hosta*.

△ *Sow your Canterbury bells alongside the wallflowers in June or buy plants in autumn. Some strains have saucers as well as cups and are sure to win admiring glances from passers-by.*

▽ *In April lift your Canterbury bells and plant them in plastic pots to grow on until the flower spikes show, or put them straight into the display pot.*

▷ *It may be unconventional, but transferring hardy annuals and biennials from borders to pots can give you a surprisingly good start to summer with enough bloom almost to conceal the container.*

Autumn

Don't panic if your pansies are a yard long, your rock daisies are brushing the ground and your grey-leaved *Helichrysum* is completely out of hand. They can redeem themselves alongside true autumn performers if you raise them on an upturned pot for extra prominence.

RECYCLING YOUR PLANTS

Leggy pansy stems can be cunningly concealed in the deep bed of foliage created by 'Red Peacock' ornamental kale and variegated *Iris*. Fill out the base with a pale yellow- or grey-leaved *Helichrysum* transplanted from a summer container. Tuck in the pansies then, as a drape, transfer a *Brachyscome* from another container and introduce some new plants such as *Sedum* 'Ruby Glow'. If you pack enough in, and give your summer bedders one last outing, I think you'll be pleasantly surprised at the end-result.

Winter

Some of the biggest, best-value evergreens available from nurseries and garden centres are field-grown conifers that have been dug up and transferred to plastic pots. Handle them only by the pot, however, as some may not have made much new root growth since their move.

PACKING THEM IN

An easy formula for a winter container is to plant three contrasting foliage plants behind two flowering varieties. Dark plum colours and reds can get lost against sombre evergreens so introduce yellow foliage to backlight them.

I filled my giant plain pot with just such a conifer – a spire-shaped, yellow Lawson cypress – which created a real shaft of sunshine and was a perfect backbone for my winter arrangement. I then leaned 'Pembury Blue' Lawson cypress (the best blue cultivar) at 45 degrees so it sprayed out over the pot edge. Don't try to use a small *Skimmia* in a giant pot of these proportions; it will only look twee. For six months of pleasure it's worth splashing out on a red-budded monster like this.

△ *Set your pot down on a paving slab or timber deck square. Even tough evergreens will appreciate a sheltered suntrap such as this out of cold, biting winds.*

◁ *Summer performers that are looking lonely and forlorn can be gathered up and packed together with autumnal plants in one roomy container to make a colourful and successful showpiece.*

WINTER RECIPE

JAN	FEB	MAR	APR	MAY	JUN
JUL	AUG	SEP	OCT	NOV	DEC

YOU WILL NEED

- 1 mature, yellow Lawson cypress (*Chamaecyparis lawsoniana* 'Golden Triumph' or similar) (1)
- 1 blue Lawson cypress (*C.l.* 'Pembury Blue' ♀) (2)
- 1 mature *Skimmia japonica* 'Rubella' ♀ (3)
- 1 *Olearia macrodonta* ♀ (4)
- 1 purple-flowered Lenten rose (*Helleborus orientalis*) (5)
- broken polystyrene chunks or crocks
- 60 litres ericaceous (lime-free) potting compost

GOOD SUBSTITUTES

Witch hazel (*Hamamelis*) would make a captivating alternative to the yellow conifer, especially if you added a frill of winter heathers at the edge of the pot.

▽ *When they have finished flowering, replace your Lenten roses with dwarf daffodils such as these dainty 'Minnow'. Fill in below with forget-me-nots to flatter the perfumed Skimmia.*

Just as a large garden demands bold gestures, so an enormous pot such as this needs large evergreens to create a balanced display.

◁ *For me container gardening is part of a cycle in which newly purchased plants are enjoyed at close quarters before being set out permanently in a border. Here, purple Lenten roses shine out among snowdrops, aconites and Crocus. Collect and sow the seed in June and you'll soon have youngsters growing on for future container creations.*

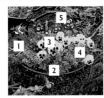
Flat-bottomed Wire Basket

Although many new products have been introduced to make life easier for the hanging basket gardener, I still prefer my flat-bottomed, wire hanging basket. Lined with moss and then plastic, it remains stable when planting, and as it holds more compost than conventional, rounded types it cut downs on the watering regime too.

Height 15cm (6in)
Diameter 40cm (16in)
Weight (when planted and watered) 12kg (26lb)

Spring

Most basket owners create only one display each year, and this is generally an eye-popping one in summer. My 'non-stop', year-round basket schedule allows for no such slacking. Spring starts with such a lavish show of bloom that I'm surprised everyone's not planting yellow-and-black pansies through streams of grape hyacinths, forget-me-nots and pink *Arabis* in containers and borders.

PLANTING TACTICS

If you have only one hanging basket and it is being used for a winter display, you will need to wait until March to start on this spring planting. Prepare by potting up the grape hyacinths (and any other bulbs you fancy) the previous autumn so they are ready to flower six months later. 'Frühlingszauber' is available in autumn and spring, as are the yellow-and-black pansies. The other plants in this basket can be home grown.

Throughout this book I recommend digging up autumn-planted forget-me-nots and Canterbury bells or self-sown golden feverfew and poached egg plants from beds and borders for use in containers. It's a bit unconventional, but you get a bigger, bushier plant with more roots. I also move my auriculas from beds to pots and back again each year and split them after flowering. Now all you have to do is plant them in the basket, do a bit of tweaking and enjoy the spectacle. If you're like me, you'll be out in the garden several times the same day to enjoy your handiwork.

▽ Position your spring medley so you can see the blooms not the bare base – whether this is nestling in the fork of an apple tree, like this, or suspended on a long chain from a sturdy bracket.

◁ It will take two or three days for the pansies to perk up after planting. You can speed this up by teasing out the flowers carefully so that they face passers-by.

△ *Small, delicate flowers and ferny foliage combine in the summer basket to give a subtle scheme that would be ruined by an outsized plant such as a Petunia.*

Summer

Diascia flowers extremely well in summer, almost to the point – as with *Nemesia denticulata* 'Confetti' – that you begin to tire of it. One of the best is *Diascia* 'Salmon Supreme' though you may need to dilute its colour with blue, white and grey.

GATHERING THE PLANTS

A good way to familiarise yourself with *Diascia* is to buy a collection of young plug plants by mail order. You can add the rock daisies to the order too. Plug plants are popular with basket enthusiasts because their tapering rootballs easily fit through the wire. Alternatively you can pot them on and add them later in the top layer.

For three years I tried to grow this cheeky little 'Bluebird' violet from seed and now that I've succeeded I intend to root cuttings and hang on to it. The plants vary in the amount of blue they exhibit so just propagate the best.

The *Tanacetum* is a gem with its grey, fern-like leaves – and hardy too if given good drainage. It's twice as refined as *Helichrysum petiolare*♀, which often dominates hanging baskets.

A basket such as this, full of small-leaved plants, is likely to tolerate the odd day or two without water, so don't worry if you're away for a weekend. Adding water-retaining granules and slow-release fertilisers will further reduce upkeep.

GRASS BASKET

If cutting the lawn is becoming a chore or it's the colour of parchment, why not plant up a matching basket of grasses that don't need trimming.

These sedges (*Carex*) (right) have great stage presence. They are *C. comans* bronze form and *C.* 'Frosted Curls' and both have an arching habit that makes them good for the top of a basket or tall oil jar. Alongside is blue fescue (*Festuca glauca* 'Elijah Blue') and at the back the variegated form of purple moor grass (*Molinia caerulea* 'Variegata'♀) – one of my top five dwarf grasses. All are clump forming.

I sat the completed flat-bottomed wire basket on a chimney pot, although it would look equally good when suspended.

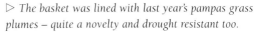

▷ *The basket was lined with last year's pampas grass plumes – quite a novelty and drought resistant too.*

Autumn

With good husbandry my summer recipe could entertain you until the frosts, but that would mean missing out on some tempting treats that only autumn can offer. Gentians for example have an aura of exclusivity. Some are a challenge to grow and flower, such as the spring-blooming *Gentiana verna*, but the late trumpet flowers typified by *G. sino-ornata* are easier. Give them a damp, acid soil and sunlight to encourage the flowers. They go well with late summer-flowering heathers.

TESTING TIMES

These miniature forms of florists' cyclamen (right) have been heavily promoted as the way to pep up flagging containers in autumn. However they were nothing like as tough as a true species such as *Cyclamen hederifolium* ♀. Their petals were prone to spotting, then the stalks rotted at the base. I suspect my florists' cyclamen were not fully hardened off when I bought them so I won't pick them from the indoor sales benches again.

In cold, wet weather, you may wish to hang this basket in a well-lit porch, or under the eaves of the house. Position it low enough to see the flowers.

△ *To maintain some continuity, retain the grey* Tanacetum *from the summer basket when you introduce new plants for autumn.*

△ *Carefully manoeuvre the Lenten rose rootball within the basket until the plant is showing its best side to the viewer.*

Winter

For a winter treat why not plant a basket like this, contrasting the Lenten rose's flowers with the supporting cast below. The best way to reveal the innermost beauty of these nodding flowers and of snowdrops is to suspend them at eye level. The basket also looked good on an upturned flower pot with the purple Lenten rose picked out against yellow-variegated leaves.

FERN LINERS

I lined the basket with a thick layer of decaying fern fronds, which are a better insulator than moss. Position your Lenten rose at the back of the basket and spin it around until you have the best spread of blooms facing forwards. Fill up half way with compost, and add the pot-grown snowdrops – dotting them about so they look as though they're self-seeded. Then add the *Cyclamen*. If you suspend the basket outdoors, try it by a sheltered window where you can enjoy it from inside.

▷ Cyclamen coum *and snowdrops contribute to a classic winter association.*

Wooden Hay Cart

If you yearn for the time when heavy horses worked the land and on golden summer days the village gathered in the harvest, you just might settle for this scaled-down version. These tiny carts are not children's toys; mine was once used to carry milk churns on a farm and makes the most appealing mobile plant stand you could ever wish for.

Height (excluding wheels) 30cm (12in)
Width 50cm (20in)
Length 70cm (28in)
Weight 15kg (33lb)

Spring

It's easy to get tunnel vision when container gardening and become bogged down in traditional gardening techniques. This hay cart is not a container in the conventional sense nor are the pots of bulbs 'planted' in the usual way. It can however be wheeled out in front of naturalised daffodils and be filled with an ever-changing selection of bulbs that give a powerful, visual link with the backdrop. When they're spent, you can move onto pots of Asiatic lilies parked alongside roses.

GOLDEN VISTAS

The range of daffodils available is mouthwatering and even tall varieties can be grown in large pots, tubs and troughs. Most will settle down happily in the garden after their stint in a container and give years of pleasure. However don't plant them out until you have separated them into individual bulbs so they can go in about 15cm (6in) apart. In due course, you could return some to pots again.

Pot up your spring bulbs in autumn, selecting varieties that will give contrasting heights and colours and either peak together like these daffodils and grape hyacinths or give a spread of interest. Hyacinths would be a joy on the patio in April, while ornamental onions such as *Allium hollandicum* 'Purple Sensation' ♀ are great fun to have around in May.

If you would prefer to start the show off earlier, in March, include the dwarf, kaufmanniana hybrid tulips such as 'Ancilla' ♀, 'Shakespeare' and 'Stresa' ♀. Mix them in with specimen-sized winter heathers for optimum effect.

◁◁ *The exciting range of daffodil sizes, shapes and colours means there are varieties for every type of situation and container.*

◁ *You don't need to wait until the bulbs are in full bloom like this before plunging them in hay – though it's a good way to check on heights and colours.*

▷ *Blaze a trail with a miniature cart topped up at regular intervals with pot-grown bulbs.*

Summer

Although this array of *Begonia* is rather brash, you may, like me, have a childlike fascination for those slightly over-the-top blooms. I just happen to like these particular flowers (in this particular setting) as much as my rare and refined honey bush (*Melianthus major*♀) and *Amicia zygomeris*.

BEGONIA BANDWAGON

All these *Begonia* are grown from dry corms potted up in April and kept in a frost-free greenhouse until mid-May. They were then gradually hardened off by being stood under a warm wall in the day and returned inside if a cold night was forecast. To encourage the corms to produce roots on their top and bottom, set them about 2.5cm (1in) below the compost level, hollow side up. Water sparingly until shoots appear. Transfer them to the hay cart when flower buds begin to show.

Encourage garden *Begonia* to produce a mass of small to medium-sized blooms, so don't pick off any single, female flowers on the doubles as you would do when cultivating a specimen *Begonia* for exhibition purposes.

◁ *Half a dozen pots filled with a single variety of plant will prove invaluable when grouping your summer containers. The yellow* Bidens *backlights the* Begonia *in a way that a red-brick wall could never do.*

Autumn

Marrows, pumpkins, squashes and gourds last longer in storage if they have first been ripened in the sun and their skins hardened, so why not flaunt them during this process. A wagonload will light up a border and provide an irresistible focal point among late annuals and perennials such as *Rudbeckia* daisies, chrysanths, ornamental kale and *Gaillardia*.

MOVABLE FEAST

You can buy a wide range of marrows, pumpkins, squashes and gourds from the greengrocer or supermarket. Better still, grow your own in beds or growing bags – training marrows and ornamental gourds up and over arches and pergolas or even onto a low roof. If you've got a big porch or hallway, bring the cart and contents indoors and set up a harvest theme.

◁ *If well ripened, ornamental gourds will last for months but you must move them indoors before the first frosts are expected.*

JAN	FEB	MAR	APR	MAY	JUN
JUL	AUG	SEP	OCT	NOV	DEC

YOU WILL NEED

- 2 Christmas box (*Sarcococca hookeriana* var. *digyna* ♀) (1)
- I yellow-variegated Japanese rush (*Acorus gramineus* 'Ogon') (2)
- 2 *Skimmia japonica* 'Rubella' ♀ (3)
- 2 yew (*Taxus baccata* ♀) (4)
- I yellow-leaved tree heather (*Erica arborea* 'Albert's Gold' ♀) (5)
- I blue Lawson cypress (*Chamaecyparis lawsoniana* 'Pembury Blue' ♀) (6)
- I blue flaky juniper (*Juniperus squamata* 'Blue Carpet' ♀) (7)
- I *Leucothoe walteri* 'Rainbow' (8)

GOOD SUBSTITUTES

There are a white-variegated form of Japanese rush and several more good Christmas box readily available.

FOR CONTINUITY

Inject more colour using pot-grown *Iris* and *Crocus*, dwarf botanical tulips and miniature daffodils concealed among the evergreen leaves. As more shrubs come into season, swap new for old.

Winter

One of the many advantages of a wheeled planter in winter is that you can trundle it under cover or near the shelter of house walls in bad weather. You could also create a two-sided display and turn it round every now and then for a change of scenery.

I had a specific viewpoint in mind when I parked the cart against the green, conservatory door. I envisaged tough evergreens forming a backdrop to more extrovert winter plants spilling over the cart sides and flowing out of the back onto the patio. Rather like a lorry that had shed its load, and the contents had then arranged themselves in a tasteful fashion!

CREATING THE DISPLAY

Contrasts of colour, form and texture are the mainstay of an exciting winter arrangement. Perfume too is important. These Christmas box flowers have a penetrating scent that belies their inconspicuous appearance. The Japanese rush has leaves spiced with ginger and cinnamon and the *Skimmia japonica* 'Rubella' produces sweetly perfumed flowers in April.

Position the tall evergreens in the rear and stack one pot on top of another to gain height if you need to. Look for a couple of drapes like this tree heather and blue Lawson cypress to sweep over the edge.

Add the front-row plants, contrasting spiky forms with broad, variegated leaves and fine, feathery needles. Let the plants flow onto the ground in a river of foliage and flower. I used the ever-reliable *Juniperus conferta* and two large winter heathers to 'anchor' the cart to the ground.

Finally, tuck in the red-budded *Skimmia*, and work hay in between the pots as a disguise and insulator to stop them freezing solid.

△ *Start off your arrangement with a 'hedge' of evergreens at the rear. Then fill in with brighter seasonal evergreens over and between the front rails.*

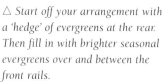
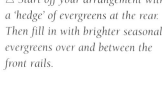

△◁ *To make the most from your container or display vehicle, always take time to move it around until it is displayed to its best advantage. Plants viewed from an angled vista such as this can result in a highly dramatic, banked-up wall of colour.*

▷ *Finish off the display by tucking in small Skimmia, hiding their pots among the spreading foliage.*

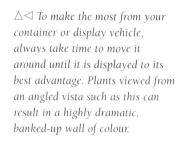

▷ *Winter need never be dull again when ideas and plants arrive by the wagonload.*

Blue Toy Chest

It's surprising what can be pressed into service as a planter. Plastic vegetable racks, bowls and even buckets are often cheaper and more individual than custom-made garden pots, though you must drill drainage holes in the base. This blue box is deep enough to retain moisture and take sizeable rootballs.

Height 28cm (11in)
Width 30cm (12in)
Length 46cm (18in)
Weight 1kg (2lb)

Spring

In spring, I sometimes yearn for the colour blue, when all around me is a blanket of yellow and white. I therefore decided that a sizeable injection of toy-chest blue was needed. For my display I paired up some gems including jewel-like tulips emerging through white strings of *Pieris* pearls.

JEWEL BOX

At the back of my chest I planted a large *Pieris* already in bud. It was not cheap, but treated well should last a lifetime. In early March, I planted pot-grown tulips, before adding an edging of grape hyacinths, pansies and periwinkle. Finally I dug up, deslugged and tidied up a clump of primroses, and added that.

△ Interplant Pieris with tulips and other spring favourites to build up a vibrant floral tapestry.

Summer

If you want some old-fashioned charm, look for cottage-garden plants such as dwarf sunflowers, pot marigolds and nasturtiums. Sow the pot marigolds and nasturtiums directly into the toy chest in April. If you would like your sunflowers to peak together and be able to grade them for height, grow them in separate pots and add them as the petals peep out. I sowed mine on 23 April and the first petals appeared during a heatwave on 23 July.

NEW HORIZONS

Using more old-fashioned plants (left), I planted up this uncompromising selection of spring and early summer flowers including poached egg plant (*Limnanthes*) and 'Jolly Joker' and 'Chantreyland' pansies with orange wallflowers and pink double daisies. Surrounded by soothing blue, you can clash orange with pink in the same display, if you dare!

▽ Guests will certainly remember their visit if you present them with this glorious outpouring of dayglo orange, yellow, purple and pink.

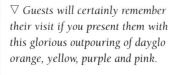

▷ Hardy annuals in this deep blue summer container have a character and poise not always evident in their half-hardy counterparts. The nasturtiums could almost be tumbling into a tropical lagoon.

Autumn

Yoder chrysanths (also sold as garden mums and cushion chrysanths) are one of the most popular plants in garden centres and nurseries in autumn. These compact, free-flowering plants are available in a kaleidoscope of colours and, given a little protection, will come through most winters unscathed. Once tried, I think you'll find it hard to imagine autumn without them.

BUYING PLANTS

You can buy fully-grown chrysanths in bud or flower and put them straight out in the garden, but some varieties are extremely brittle and shed side shoots before you get them home. These 'Harvest Emily' arrived by post in spring. I potted them up immediately into 9cm (3½in) pots and then put them in an unheated greenhouse.

To cultivate dome-shaped plants and coax them into flower, plant them in at least a 13cm (5in) pot, pinch out their shoot tips frequently and feed regularly. Stand them in the garden in a sunny, well-lit spot from May onwards, and with careful handling they should thrive.

COMPANION PLANTING

Columbine may seem an unlikely partner for an autumn-flowering plant, as it has flowered by July. There is however a new generation of foliage plants with leaves that are yellow, bronze or flecked with green, pale green and yellow. Being seed raised, there is much variation among them and my packet of 'Roman Bronze' produced some interesting mutations, all worth growing.

They were sown in February and stood outside to chill. Then after six weeks I moved them to the propagator. By September they looked elegant between 'Harvest Emily' blooms. They flowered the following year – deep violet, pink and blue.

Another novel tender perennial is *Centradenia*, a trailer sold as a young plant or plug. The pink flowers are welcome, though fleeting. The real display begins as the foliage takes on burnished tones in summer and autumn.

△ *When each chrysanthemum reaches 7.5–10cm (3–4in) high, pinch out its leader to encourage bushy, compact growth instead of flower-bud formation. Repeat this operation on the resulting stems and once again after this. You can let flower buds develop from July onwards.*

▷ *This autumn adventure lifts the lid on three plants that other container gardeners are unlikely to have combined before. Half the fun is in creating something unique.*

Winter

The early months of the year are perhaps the most difficult for container gardeners to tackle with real enthusiasm. Severe weather may freeze plants solid so it's impossible to arrange them and even, at times, get water into their rootballs without bringing them indoors first to thaw out.

Even in January however there are mild spells when you can create a spectacle or two. Winter heathers are getting into their stride and there are plenty of other contenders with leaf and berry colour to put alongside them.

FRONT ROW

This arrangement calls for three plants to fill out the front of the chest and spill over the lip, so when you're buying hold each plant up to see if it spreads over the pot rim. If it does, it's likely to be one of the most useful shapes for pot work.

A good tip is to try out your front row line-up on the floor and pick out the permutation that works best. Contrast in texture and colour are important to make a lively show.

Look out for sizeable plants too, especially with heathers. One specimen-sized, mature plant for example will be far more convincing than three smaller ones planted close together. I couldn't resist this silver-variegated *Euonymus*, nor the variegated form of London Pride, which seems to be as vigorous as the plain-leaved one.

PLANTING UP

There's no need to leave room around the plants for growth as there won't be any unless you plan to make your display more permanent. That's the beauty of winter containers. Any uncertainty about heights, colours and spreads becomes irrelevant because what you see is what you get. You may however like to leave a few small gaps for bulbs.

Get the back row plants in first. In the far corner, plant your tallest specimen. A green or yellow, dwarf conifer is a good choice for this key position. Then, stepping down in height, add the *Osmanthus* and pernettya, packing ericaceous potting compost around the rootballs as you go.

Finally, adjust the front row, angling the plants forward slightly so they are not overhung by the evergreens behind, and position the planter in a sheltered, sunny site.

△ *A generous boxful of coloured leaves, berries and heather flowers will keep up your spirits until the first bulbs appear.*

◁ *A rosette-leaved plant such as this variegated London pride will add variety to your front row among the fine-textured heather and* Euonymus.

WINTER RECIPE

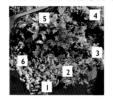

JAN	FEB	MAR	APR	MAY	JUN
JUL	AUG	SEP	OCT	NOV	DEC

YOU WILL NEED

- ⟶ 1 mature winter heather (*Erica carnea* 'Pink Spangles' ♀) (1)
- ⟶ 1 variegated *Euonymus fortunei* 'Harlequin' (2)
- ⟶ 1 variegated London Pride (*Saxifraga* x *urbium* 'Variegata') (3)
- ⟶ 1 dwarf cypress (*Chamaecyparis obtusa* 'Nana Aurea' ♀) (4)
- ⟶ 1 variegated *Osmanthus heterophyllus* 'Goshiki' (5)
- ⟶ 1 pernettya in fruit (*Gaultheria mucronata* 'Pink Pearl' ♀) (6)
- ⟶ broken polystyrene chunks or crocks
- ⟶ 40 litres ericaceous (lime-free) potting compost

GOOD SUBSTITUTES

The conifer *Thuja occidentalis* 'Rheingold' ♀ deserves a place in every winter garden. Although expensive, *Skimmia japonica* subsp. *reevesiana* is uniquely endowed with pyramids of red berries that last well into spring.

FOR CONTINUITY

Tuck in dwarf *Iris reticulata* ♀ and *I. danfordiae* and the earliest *Crocus* such as *C. ancyrensis* and *C. tommasinianus* ♀ between the evergreen edge. They'll shine out far better than in a border of bare soil. Plant the 'Pink Pearl' in a peaty bed in March near a male or hermaphrodite form of pernettya so you get another crop of berries.

ALTERNATIVELY

For other ways to make the most of winter heathers see pages 59 and 117.

Antiqued Concrete Urn

This urn boasts crisp, elegant, classical motifs and an antiqued finish – a great improvement on early versions with their poorly defined decoration and visible seams. The bowl and base separate and there is also a tall plinth to provide more height. Urns can be unstable so should not be introduced into a garden where children may clamber on them.

Height 48cm (19in)
Diameter 45cm (18in)
Weight 40kg (88lb)

Spring

If you want to sustain a generous quantity of planting for several months, you'll need an urn at least as large as my antiqued one. Volume of soil is more critical than size or shape and some urns are just too small for anything but drought-tolerant succulents. To create a greater impact select a wide-bowled urn rather than a narrow, egg-cup-shaped one.

WORD ASSOCIATIONS

At the mention of spring greens, many gardeners think of cabbages but I connect the words with a late-flowering tulip called 'Spring Green', which is so unusual that it's worth a setting all on its own. Its perfect partner is the beautifully scented 'Sir Winston Churchill' daffodil, with compatible colour, height and flowering time. I potted them both up in October and in spring put in some twiggy supports from *Eucalyptus* tree prunings. I edged up with variegated lemon balm and *Helichrysum petiolare* 'Limelight'.

△ *To add that little element of magic, we forced damp moss into the clefts around the bowl rim, as if the urn had stood in some damp hollow for a century or more. As you'll see on the next spread, once it had got a foothold, it never looked back!*

◁ *A little support will be needed for these top-heavy blooms, especially after rain, so cut some twiggy sticks to use as crutches.*

▷ *A distinctive tulip such as 'Spring Green' can be used to set up a unique colour theme that looks as vibrant and fresh as spring itself.*

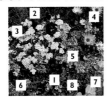
Summer

Mail order companies thrive on so-called 'tender perennials' and up-market bedders such as *Lotus*, *Osteospermum* and *Brachyscome*, selling them as young rooted cuttings in plug form or as larger plants in peat pots. Looking behind the scenes, I know some excellent new varieties are coming soon.

In their eagerness to expand their range, however, some companies have introduced plants that are clearly not suited to the great outdoors. *Acalypha* is extremely vulnerable to cold weather, *Centradenia* produces very short-lived flowers, *Tradescantia* × *andersoniana* 'Maiden's Blush' is prone to scorch and only an eternal optimist would attempt *Caladium* outdoors in a temperate climate. However when tender perennials are good, there is nothing else to touch them – as I discovered with my summer urn.

NEW-WAVE PERENNIALS

I've cheated a bit because in this summer planter I included *Salvia* × *superba* and yellow yarrow, which are hardy perennials, but who cares when they tone in so well. *S.* × *s.* 'Mainacht' makes a fine thrusting background for any large container and contrasts well with the more rounded form of the variegated daisy *Osteospermum* 'Giles Gilbey', which tends to flower in flushes with a wait of several weeks in between. You can let the *Nemesia* run into the daisies and yarrow as their flowers are a perfect colour match.

Helichrysum petiolare 'Limelight' is a better edging plant than the straight, silver-leaved *H. petiolare*♛, as it is less likely to overrun the display, and grey-leaved New Zealand burr looks pretty with white and pink water hyssop. You can reuse the *Helichrysum* from the spring recipe and buy all the other plants in May or June.

△ *Create a glow with an uncompromising flash of yellow leaves and flowers including pansies, yellow-leaved tree heather, meadowsweet, creeping Jenny and dwarf grasses.*

◁ *This soft colour scheme will soak up all the sunlight going so give it your hottest spot.*

Autumn

Autumn is the season when you are most likely to see reckless clashes of primary colours so it's good therapy to bathe your eyes occasionally in a soft pool of pastels. Long-running summer bedders and late-developing herbaceous perennials can be woven together like this to pile on the colour until the first cold snap.

Pink busy lizzies take on an air of refinement when buoyed up and diluted by blue pansies, crispy white pearl everlasting and the pink form of *Brachyscome*. Another useful plant for edging is this annual, pink baby's breath as it can readily be moved from one arrangement to another.

ENHANCING THE SETTING

Flatter the urn by manoeuvring other container-grown plants such as blue spruce (*Picea*), grey-leaved juniper, silver wormwood (*Artemisia*) and a Japanese maple (*Acer japonica*) into the picture to hint at things to come.

◁ *Busy lizzies look far better among other autumn container plants than in an urn all to themselves.*

Winter

I, like most gardeners, am sorely tempted by any new plant, but you do not always have to introduce different varieties to create an eye-catching container garden. For my winter recipe I therefore decided to use plants that had already appeared elsewhere in this book. Such repetition is unlikely to be immediately apparent because on each occasion the plants have assumed different personalities in their new containers and settings.

EVERGREEN BACKDROP

It would be hard to find three more appealing evergreen foliage plants than curry plant, Japanese cedar and *Euonymus fortunei* 'Emerald 'n' Gold' to form the backbone of a winter recipe. They also fold themselves around the tiny *Cyclamen coum* in a protective embrace. One big potful of winter heather should fill out the front of the antiqued urn.

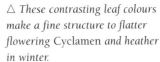

△ *These contrasting leaf colours make a fine structure to flatter flowering Cyclamen and heather in winter.*

▷ *With a bit of luck you should be able to pick up all these plants or something similar from a good garden centre or nursery.*

YOU WILL NEED

- 10 tall, mixed wallflowers (*Erysimum*) (1)
- 6 dwarf, blue forget-me-nots (*Myosotis*) (2)
- 3 blue-and-white, bicoloured, winter pansies (3)
- 10 early, single tulips (*Tulipa* 'Generaal de Wet') (4)
- 10 early double tulips (*T.* 'Schoonoord') (5)
- 20 poppy anemones (*Anemone coronaria* De Caen Group) (6)
- 1 purple-leaved bugle (*Ajuga reptans* 'Atropurpurea' ♀) (7)
- 20 grape hyacinths (*Muscari armeniacum* ♀) (8)
- broken polystyrene chunks or crocks
- 50 litres multipurpose potting compost

GOOD SUBSTITUTES

To scale down the display you could choose *Tulipa linifolia* Batalinii Group 'Bright Gem', dwarf 'Prince Mixed' wallflowers, *Anemone blanda* ♀ and violets.

FOR CONTINUITY

Plant out all the bulbs in a warm, sunny spot among spurge (*Euphorbia*), flowering quince (*Chaenomeles*), *Spiraea japonica* 'Goldflame' ♀ and Corsican hellebore (*Helleborus argutifolius* ♀).

ALTERNATIVELY

For a more contrived colour scheme that features the fiery 'Stresa' ♀ tulip see page 123.

Ceramic Pot Nest

Many containers look best in clusters and for a fully co-ordinated collection these matching, frost-proof, ceramic pots are the ideal starting point. Their speckled finish looks especially good on a bed of gravel. Be wary however of containers with garish glazes and over-decorated designs that upstage the plants.

Spring

This mixture of spring bulbs and bedding is not only highly colourful but also manages to capture the very essence of the romantic flower garden. Character, poise, perfume and cottage-garden charm are all part of the formula. Mixed colours will also often succeed in spring especially if they include soothing go-betweens such as wallflowers and forget-me-nots that rarely clash with bulbs and pansies. Such containers will look twice as impressive when positioned against coloured foliage plants.

COORDINATING THE DISPLAY

If you plant up your bulbs and wallflowers in black plastic pots in autumn, you can include the best specimens in your nest of ceramic pots in spring and perhaps select wallflowers that pick up the colour of the tulip petals.

Should you prefer a more haphazard approach, however, plant the ingredients direct into the ceramic pots in autumn: bareroot wallflowers first, then the forget-me-nots, pansies, poppy anemones, bugle and grape hyacinths and finally the tulip bulbs in between. The deliciously scented 'Generaal de Wet' tulips look wonderful with wallflowers, and 'Schoonoord' tulips are also stunners, especially with yellow and blue.

In descending sizes

Height	Diameter
30cm (12in)	33cm (13in)
25cm (10in)	25cm (10in)
23cm (9in)	21.5cm (8½in)
19cm (7½in)	20cm (8in)
15cm (6in)	15cm (6in)
Total weight 22kg (48lb)	

△ *For a change, limit the colours to red and white by underplanting Mexican orange blossom (Choisya 'Aztec Pearl' ♀) with blood-red Anemone coronaria De Caen Group 'Hollandia' and edge up with blowsy, red buttercups (Ranunculus asiaticus 'Accolade').*

▷ *Nests of ceramic pots are perfect to host a co-ordinated display of spring bulbs and bedding.*

▷ *Build up the picture by introducing French marigolds around the base of your* Dahlia *and pansy pot.*

Summer

If you associate *Dahlia* with the last half of summer and autumn, you may find it unnerving to see them flowering in June and early July at your garden centre. These plants have been forced into bloom in order to promote a new generation of patio *Dahlia*, such as the beguiling 'München', which grows only 30–45cm (12–18in) tall. I bought mine on impulse, from a range of sturdy, compact but large-flowered varieties. It was a marvellous discovery for a container and took pride of place in the largest of the ceramic pots, with pansies at its feet.

HEIGHTENING THE DRAMA

Sometimes it's tempting to introduce something dramatic and new. 'Brunig' pansies for example exhibit one of the most electric colour contrasts in the plant kingdom and they never look more scintillating than when cutting through the rich yellow flowers of *Dahlia* 'München' and 'Water Colours Mixed' pansies. As a groundwork (and to conceal the plain rim of the pot) I planted small rooted chunks of yellow heath pearlwort. They soon knitted together and helped to prop up the pansies as well.

If you like this colour scheme and don't want to force your dwarf, yellow *Dahlia* under glass, pot up the tuber in April and let it grow on under a warm wall. Sow the pansies in early May, as March-sown plants can become tall and leggy by July. Varieties that react badly to summer heat are especially vulnerable.

BEGONIA OPTION

If you prefer an orange colour scheme to a yellow one, then fill a pot with 'Non Stop' *Begonia*. You can buy corms of orange-flowered varieties separately in spring. Add clear blue or yellow pansies and as much *Lobelia* as you can fit in. Double *L. erinus* 'Kathleen Mallard' and single *L.* 'Azurea' are two decidedly upmarket varieties for your collection. Meanwhile *Tagetes* 'Starfire' can be relied upon to liven things up alongside.

△ *Blue and pink pools of* Lobelia *encircling strident orange* Begonia *flowers lend a cool, calming influence to the scene.*

Autumn

Plants that tolerate the occasional missed watering are invaluable especially to the container gardener. The resurrection plant does what it promises, and you can buy it as a dried-up brown rosette in a plastic bag from a garden centre or 'in the green' as a growing plant. It does well outdoors in summer in a shady corner.

SHADE-LOVING PLANTS

New Guinea busy lizzies thrive in the company of resurrection plant, as does *Lobelia* and with a little landscaping you can turn a problem, shady site into quite a feature. I thought the birds would appreciate the pebble-and-water-filled dishes, but it was wasps that turned up most frequently to take a drink and cool off. All these plants will appreciate a light overhead spray after the sun has gone down.

◁ *Tiny clay pavers and pebbles laid around plant saucers will create interesting patterns and textures at the front of an autumn display.*

AUTUMN RECIPE

JAN	FEB	MAR	APR	MAY	JUN
JUL	AUG	SEP	OCT	NOV	DEC

YOU WILL NEED

- 4 resurrection plants (*Selaginella lepidophylla*) (1)
- 3 variegated busy lizzies (*Impatiens* New Guinea Group 'Eurema') (2)
- 1 pink busy lizzie (*I.* New Guinea Group 'Maui') (3)
- 1 *Lobelia* 'Azurea' (4)
- 1 variegated mind-your-own-business (*Soleirolia soleirolii* 'Variegata') (5)
- broken polystyrene chunks or crocks
- 40 litres multipurpose potting compost

Winter

Conifers and heathers in island beds look a little dated nowadays, though they can work well together in winter containers, especially some of the more rugged conifers such as juniper. Introduce a framework of these into your nest of pots and then insert seasonal plants such as red-budded *Skimmia* and golden *Euonymus* among the evergreen backdrop. Alternatively in your potted winter garden you could include acid-loving heathers and early flowering, dwarf bulbs – such as *Iris reticulata*♀ and any of the kaufmanniana tulips – with enough height to rise above the carpeting evergreens.

LARGER FLOWERS

To liven things up in February, tuck in some early, pot-grown primroses among the evergreen foliage. Leave the primroses in their pots so that, if severe weather is forecast, they can be pulled out again and kept in a cool room. To keep the plants healthy, pick off spent flowers and yellowing leaves before they start to rot in the primrose crown.

◁ *Conifers and heathers are at their most valuable in winter and are especially useful to provide a framework around spring bulbs.*

WINTER RECIPE

JAN	FEB	MAR	APR	MAY	JUN
JUL	AUG	SEP	OCT	NOV	DEC

YOU WILL NEED

- 1 rounded flaky juniper (*Juniperus squamata* 'Blue Star'♀) (1)
- 1 Chinese juniper (*J. chinensis* 'Variegated Kaizaku') (2)
- 1 grey-leaved juniper (*J. virginiana* 'Grey Owl'♀) (3)
- 1 prostrate flaky juniper (*J. squamata* 'Blue Carpet'♀) (4)
- 1 Lawson cypress (*Chamaecyparis lawsoniana* 'Tharandtensis Caesia' or similar) (5)
- 1 yellow-leaved tree heather (*Erica arborea* 'Estrella Gold'♀) (6)
- broken polystyrene chunks or crocks
- 50 litres ericaceous (lime-free) potting compost

Shallow Baskets

For non-stop container displays that are quick and easy to change, these plastic-lined willow baskets are invaluable. They are light and easy to lift onto tabletops and have an air of rustic informality that should be reflected in exuberant planting schemes spilling out over the rims.

LARGE BASKET
Height 18cm (7in)
Diameter 43cm (17in)
Weight 1.5kg (3lb)

SMALL BASKET
Height 15cm (6in)
Diameter 38cm (15in)
Weight 1kg (2lb)

Spring

The difference between a good and bad gardener, they say, is two weeks and when your hyacinths have toppled over through lack of support you feel as though you've quite literally let them down. All was not lost though, for I used mine horizontally in the large basket to make a river that flowed through glowing coals and licking flames generated by 'Stresa' tulips and red hot primroses. Such a fire and water scheme both stimulates and refreshes the jaded gardener.

ALL-WEATHER TULIPS

Some tulips such as *T. tarda*♀ and *T. humilis* don't open their petals unless the sun blazes down. These 'Stresa' tulips however are almost as showy on the outside of the petals as the inside so you can enjoy them even on dull days.

Pot up the tulips and hyacinths in autumn. At the same time dig up and pot a clump of blue lungwort or buy a plant in spring. In March track down the primroses and assemble the basket, allowing each variety to drift through its neighbour.

GO NATIVE

For a far more modest gathering try this enchanting selection of native or near-native plants (right). *Viola*, primroses (*Primula vulgaris*), snake's head fritillary (*Fritillaria meleagris*♀), cowslips (*Primula veris*♀) and purple-leaved spurge (*Euphorbia*) bring a flavour of the cornfield, the damp flower meadow and the hedgebank into your garden.

△ *Tiny arrangements such as this of spring-flowering natives can be totally beguiling.*

▷ *Introduce two-tone tulips for a fiery theme, then cool it down with plenty of blue. Back up the basket with other containers so it really stands out.*

◁ *It's hard to fail with top-quality ingredients such as these for the spring basket.*

Summer

'Always hunt down the best possible variety of a plant on your must-have list'. This is one of the most valuable pieces of gardening advice I have ever been given and I hope a little of that philosophy is evident in this summer basket of relatively new (or new to me) and improved half-hardy annuals.

A PINK PATCH

The *Petunia*, tobacco plants and busy lizzies arrived as young plug plants by mail order in April. Buying plants at this state of maturity avoids the need to maintain sufficiently high germination and growing temperatures for seedlings in February and March; it will probably also give your summer containers a head start over home-grown ones. Later starters however should carry on flowering well into September, by which time those precocious, early displays may well be past their prime or been discarded.

PROGRESS REPORT

By late July, the double *Petunia* was coming into its prime, and the love-lies-bleeding was looking bright and bushy tailed and toning in well with the pink theme. I thinned out the busy lizzies and used the spares in another display.

BLOSSOM TIME

Given the vagaries of the weather and predation by pests and diseases, it's sometimes difficult to ensure that a display will peak at a preplanned or convenient time, despite your best efforts to stage manage the show.

In early July my basket was definitely peaking, with the nodding 'Havana Appleblossom' tobacco plants at their best. This dwarf variety, with its pink, shy, drooping flowers, has won a fleuroselect gold medal (the plant equivalent of an Olympic Gold) and looked wonderful with pink and white, double *Petunia* and the beetroot tones of *Amaranthus hypochondriacus* 'Red Fox' – a particularly dark form of love-lies-bleeding. From this stage onwards, with the basket full of roots, regular feeding was needed to encourage more growth and flower buds.

REWARDING RESULTS

I used both willow baskets for this alternative summer creation (far left), which by late June was looking spectacular. I bought the delicate *Schizanthus*. The large-flowered Canterbury bells and cornflowers were sown the previous year in a border and transplanted, the red and white *Nemesia strumosa* 'National Ensign' was sown in April and the trailing bellflower and lady's mantle were taken from my potted nursery.

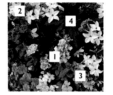
◁ *As a season progresses, the emphasis between the various plants in a container may well change. Early July saw the most prolific outpouring of bloom in my summer basket. Later, the love-lies-bleeding became more prominent, as you can see from the picture at the top of this page.*

◁◁ *Although it's time consuming to create complex arrangements such as this, your level of job satisfaction afterwards will be immeasurably greater.*

Autumn

If you fancy a change of scenery by August or September you can discard or relocate the bedding plants from the summer recipe, leaving only *Amaranthus hypochondriacus* 'Red Fox'. *Celosia spicata* 'Pink Flamingo' proved ideal to bring up the rear of the basket in what was the most strikingly modern set-piece of the year.

NON-STOP ACTION

Plant the *Celosia* in a semi-circle around the love-lies-bleeding, then, to hide all those bare stems, work in the succulent ice plants. They look good even before the flower buds are formed and are virtually guaranteed to attract the ultimate plant accessory when they do flower – tortoiseshell butterflies. I mulched the surface with fir cones as a finishing touch.

DRIED FLOWERS

Cut the love-lies-bleeding and *Celosia* flowers, dry them and arrange them with more traditional strawflowers (*Helichrysum bracteatum*), ornamental grasses and statice (*Limonium*) for an indoor display that will give pleasure for months on end. Shake out some black seeds from the *Celosia* to sow the following year.

△▷ *Strip out the summer busy lizzies, Petunia and tobacco plants, leaving the 'Red Fox' as the nucleus for the autumn basket.*

▷ *Add the unusual, seed-raised* Celosia *at the back of the autumn basket and ice plants along the front.*

Winter

Sedum 'Herbstfreude' is truly a plant for all seasons. It looks good from the moment its paddle-shaped, succulent leaves nose through the soil in spring. Not only has it an extended flowering season but it also produces marvellous, burnished seedheads. When featured alongside other winter skeletons, adventurous gardeners will appreciate the attraction of delaying the deadheading until early spring. Moreover, brown-leaved sedges are all the rage now, even though at times it's hard to tell if they're still alive.

Brown willow baskets are the perfect venue for such a winter creation. I gave mine a thick mulch of hay and perched it on a convenient branch in front of a boundary hedge.

◁ *The modest beauty in the burnished and bleached remains of stonecrops, sedges and* Persicaria *persists all winter long.*

▷ *Build up a picture frame around your autumn basket by suspending Petunia 'Purple Wave' and busy lizzies from a beam or bracket and moving in seasonal plants as their leaves colour up.*

JAN	FEB	MAR	APR	MAY	JUN
JUL	AUG	SEP	OCT	NOV	DEC

YOU WILL NEED

- 5 blue, yellow-eyed primroses (1)
- 5 'Royal Delft' pansies (2)
- 20 grape hyacinths (*Muscari armeniacum* ♀) (3)
- broken polystyrene chunks or crocks
- 13 litres multipurpose potting compost
- Cotswold chippings for topdressing

GOOD SUBSTITUTES

Muscari latifolium boasts two-tone, blue and violet flowers and broad leaves, while a white-flowered *Muscari* would pick up the pansy petals. 'Maxim Marina' and 'Joker Light Blue' pansies are both good varieties with darker, less whiskery faces than 'Royal Delft'.

FOR CONTINUITY

Dig up the grape hyacinths and primroses and combine them with dwarf daffodils in a damp bed in sun or semi-shade. Lift out the pansies and recycle them or leave them *in situ* for another planting scheme.

ALTERNATIVELY

For another primrose-inspired creation see page 131.

▷ *Grape hyacinths and primroses are on parade again in this striking concoction of colours.*

Simulated-stone Trough

Wider than a windowbox, this cast, concrete trough can accommodate three formal lines of plants as well as informally positioned dwarf shrubs and bedding. It looks good with blue flowers and complements buff-coloured slabs, walls and Cotswold chippings. Two people are needed to lift the trough as it is so heavy.

Height 23cm (9in)
Width 23cm (9in)
Length 43cm (17in)
Weight 30kg (66lb)

Spring

If you're searching for a theme or colour scheme for your spring container, why not base it on the many colours and varieties of primrose. Most are bicolours. To complement my blue, yellow-eyed primroses I introduced blue-winged, yellow-eyed, white-petalled pansies and bright blue, white-mouthed grape hyacinths.

Before you start planting tidy up the primroses by removing any yellow or rotting leaves. They are much harder to reach when you've finished. I positioned the primroses towards the edge of the trough with their leaves curling over the rim, and added pansies interplanted with pot-grown grape hyacinths. If you've space you could put tall polyanthus at the back to bank up the colour. Finally I covered any bare soil with Cotswold chippings, which look good and also deter slugs.

△ *There are some sumptuous selections of primroses to tempt you. They range from the dark-leaved 'Wanda' hybrids, single colours with a small contrasting eye, to large-flowered bicolours and the suffused types that lighten in colour towards the tips of the petals.*

SHOP AROUND

It's well worth looking through the sales benches in early spring to see if there are any unusual colours worth picking out. Large DIY outlets and garden centre chains tend to carry the same range of bedding at each store, so it may be in the smaller town and country nurseries that you find the unexpected. I've bought excellent polyanthus root-wrapped with damp newspaper.

These glorious pink, yellow and ginger primrose selections make unusual and telling companions to grape hyacinths (left). After flowering plant them out in May and let them mature for use the following year.

▷ *It would be hard to devise a more suitable colour scheme than this for a buff-coloured trough or pot. Remove the pansies though and you'd lose more than half the impact, such is their charisma.*

Summer

Tuberous *Begonia* can be almost as fascinating and sophisticated as *Pelargonium* so it is worth taking the trouble to seek out rare, unusual and desirable varieties such as *Begonia* 'Switzerland' (dark leaves and rich red flowers), *B. sutherlandii*♥ (trailing, small orange blooms) or the subtle tones of these *B.* 'Bertinii'. They can be potted up in March and grown on as you would any other tuberous type, though you may need to order them from the spring catalogue of a specialist bulb supplier.

It would be easy to overpower these pastel tones with dominant primary colours so I used a pansy of similar complexion to make a perfect marriage and a *Lobelia* to sprinkle confetti at their feet.

▷ Begonia *with a pronounced eye have more character than blowsy doubles and they also look good alongside cheeky pansy blooms.*

▽ *If you prefer single to double flowers you may also wish to seek out these* Begonia Crispa Marginata. *Their flowers go superbly with striped and ruffled* Petunia *and dark-leaved, red* Dahlia *such as 'Bishop of Llandaff'.*

PERFECT TIMING

You'll need to grow the *Begonia*, pansies and *Lobelia* yourself for none is likely to be available as plants from garden centres. If you get your timing right, all these plants will develop at a similar rate and each will take its allocated place in a three-row line-up.

Firstly, sow the *Lobelia* in heat in February or early March, but don't cover the seed, and prick out into clumps not individual seedlings. Pot up the *Begonia* tubers in March and sow the pansies at the same time. In early June, plant up your simulated-stone trough with the *Begonia* at the back interplanted with the pansies, then edge up the front and down the sides with *Lobelia*.

Autumn

The imaginative use of plants is fundamental to a successful container display. Every plant has at least one natural partner and the art of gardening lies in the success of the whole rather than the pursuit of perfection in any individual species. Occasionally however you may decide to be more single-minded and plant one variety on its own to create a truly memorable, eye-catching display. The *Aster* in my autumn recipe has done just this.

SINGLE SPOTLIGHT

Aster will make a lively end to the bedding display when other annuals are flagging. You can buy dwarf varieties in pots in summer or sow seed in April or May for a late-summer spectacular.

◁ *Aster 'Teisa Stars' is the best dwarf variety I've grown. It looks good alone (as in this autumn trough) or with coneflowers such as Rudbeckia 'Becky Mixed'.*

Winter

The colours yellow and gold are well illustrated by the contrasts these yellow daffodils make with the burnished, 'old gold' tints of 'Rheingold' conifer and the more gold than yellow, hybrid *Crocus* 'Yellow Giant'. This subtle variation will spice up a single-colour theme in late winter, especially if you also include these voluptuous yellow, orange-centred primroses.

I planted the *Crocus* in plastic half-pots in November and bought the double-headed 'Jumblie' daffodils and the primroses in February.

◁ *With a little planning, you can have this late winter recipe up and running in an instant.*

Giant Decorated Pot

Few containers are more spectacular than this beautifully decorated, swag-and-acanthus-leaved pot. Mine has been five years in the weathering and is large enough to be almost an elevated garden in itself. Such decorated pots are not cheap but are frost proof and likely to become family heirlooms.

Height 48cm (19in)
Diameter 58cm (23in)
Weight 50kg (110lb)

Spring

Throughout *Non-Stop Containers* I have used supporting plants and props to frame a star performer. A nest of complementary planting – with an occasional eye-catcher – builds up a picture, whereas even a tastefully planted container can lose half its impact when sited on a bare, concrete patio.

In the next few pages you'll find many ideas on framing your giant pot, building a plinth for it and laying on a continuous feast of colour whatever the weather. There is no need to strip the pot bare every season as the two trailing conifers in this spring recipe are retained from the winter pot.

SPRING SELECTION

A particularly good, tall daffodil makes a fine centrepiece for an outsized pot and these 'Changing Colours' are both subtle and showy. You'll certainly get a grandstand view of the flowers by raising them up to this height, and – even if they tend to nod over – carefully chosen, front-row planting will give them a little support. Other outstanding plants to look for in garden centres and nurseries include 'Fens Ruby' cypress spurge and *Veronica peduncularis* 'Georgia Blue'.

For a one-sided display like mine, put the daffodils in at the back, then underplant with the perennial wallflower and cypress spurge. Tuck in the speedwell between the two existing conifers and you are set up until late May.

LATE DEVELOPERS

As the daffodils fade, the gentian-blue speedwell starts into bloom and looks lovely against the lime-green cypress spurge. 'Fens Ruby' is a treasure in pots. Its lime-green flowers take on pink tinges as they fade among ruby shoot tips. By this time the wallflower will be peaking.

▷ *Gather a variety of spring ingredients together to see which co-ordinate best with the two conifers retained from the winter pot (see pages 138–9).*

◁ *Once the daffodils are passed their best, the spotlight will switch to the blue speedwell.*

▷▷ *Tiny clay pavers and pebbles add prominence to the decorated terracotta pot. This would be a clever way to disguise dull paving slabs too.*

Summer

Tens of thousands of dwarf, pot-grown lilies are snapped up each year by gardeners hungry for summer colour. One of the bestselling varieties is the orange-flowered *Lilium* 'Enchantment' ♥, though it's not the easiest colour to place. 'Mona Lisa' is more soothing on the eye and is also blessed with such a penetrating perfume that I decided a special setting was called for.

FIRST IMPRESSIONS

Are your visitors welcomed by an arrangement of the season's finest – or is the reality unyielding tarmac or block paving? One large container such as this could trigger a remarkable transformation.

Even if you start your summer display as late as July, you'll still find lilies and *Aster* for sale in pots. Alternatively pot up your lily tubers in March or April and sow *Aster* seed in April. To flatter their flowers I wove in some decoratively coloured foliage. Variegated bugle, granny's bonnets and tall cardinal flowers all produce interesting leaves as well as flowers. The first two also bridge the gap between spring and summer, so are doubly valuable to a gardener.

MAKING A PLINTH

An elevated platform will protect your precious pot from bumps and add an air of grandeur. To make this plinth, lay eight granite setts and eight bricks alternately in a square, with a granite sett at each corner and the bricks standing on their sides. Then lay four more granite setts against the central sett in each side. Mortar everything in position if it is likely to become dislodged. Then fill the centre with gravel.

When finished, get help to manoeuvre the giant decorated pot into position. To deter someone from stealing a large, expensive container, put half a dozen more bricks in its base to increase the weight.

△ *Gather a selection of cut flowers and leaves to see which will make good companions for your lilies.*

△ *You don't need large, deep pots to grow good lilies. Pot up dwarf varieties in individual pots and larger ones two or three per 18cm (7in) pot. Transfer them to your display container when the flower buds show.*

◁ *A fine pot deserves a special plinth to sit on. This one can be made quickly and simply, with no special bricklaying skills.*

▷ *Once the plinth and planted pot are in place, build up the frame with spreading evergreens and a backdrop of coloured leaves.*

Autumn

To create an autumn border, delay sowing *Cosmos*, *Zinnia* and coneflowers (*Rudbeckia*) until May. Plant them out among *Dahlia*, cardinal flowers and *Salvia patens*♀, leaving the odd paving slab here and there as the base for a sizeable pot. Each container will provide a focal point within the border. Behind the display pots, plunge some container-grown trees and shrubs that are renowned for their autumn tints.

BUILDING A BACKDROP

A tall, variegated cabbage palm (*Cordyline*) gives height and drama to the backdrop border (bottom right) while *Cosmos* flowers try to out-perform the giant decorated pot in the left-hand corner of the picture. Variegated *Miscanthus* grass, castor oil plant (*Ricinus communis*) and honey bush

△ *Most Cosmos are a little too boisterous for containers, but you can still enjoy them as a backdrop with pink* Dahlia, *tall Japanese anemone and exotic, cut-leaved honey bush.*

(*Melianthus major*) will flourish in pots or a border. The molten-leaved, sweet gum (*Liquidamber styraciflua*) takes several weeks to reach its full, screaming scarlet.

△ *Cosmos never forms a dense mass of flowers, but only a hard frost will curb its hyperactive production of buds.*

▷ *Why let your garden run to seed in autumn when you could lay on a spectacular late border show as good as this.*

◁ *A well-placed pot set in an autumnal border that is coming to its peak will give an almost seamless wall of brilliant leaf and flower colour.*

AUTUMN RECIPE

JAN	FEB	MAR	APR	MAY	JUN
JUL	AUG	SEP	OCT	NOV	DEC

YOU WILL NEED

- 2 Japanese anemone (*Anemone hupehensis* 'Splendens') (1)
- 1 *Euonymus japonicus* 'Aureus' (2)
- 2 ornamental kale (one pink and one purple) (3)
- 2 pinky purple, dwarf michaelmas daisies (*Aster novi-belgii* 'Lady in Blue') (4)
- 2 deep pink, dwarf michaelmas daisies (*A. n.-b.* 'Little Pink Beauty') (5)
- 1 lilyturf (*Liriope muscari* 'Gold-banded') (6)
- 1 *Diascia* 'Salmon Supreme' (7)
- broken polystyrene chunks or crocks
- 60 litres multipurpose potting compost

GOOD SUBSTITUTES

Liriope exiliflora 'Ariaka-janshige', syn. 'Silvery Sunproof', is a better, more vigorous variegated form than *L. muscari* 'Gold-banded'. *Aster amellus* 'Veilchenkönigen'♀, syn. 'Violet Queen', is a treasure and less prone to mildew than *A. novi-belgii* varieties. If you can't buy good-quality Japanese anemones substitute dwarf chrysanths.

FOR CONTINUITY

Familiarise yourself with new herbaceous plants by growing them in containers where you can enjoy them at close quarters before planting them out permanently in a border.

Winter

A winter pot filled with plants that tolerate severe weather will last considerably longer than one containing forced primroses, dwarf daffodils and pansies, which might survive only in very sheltered areas. For my winter display I therefore settled on a yellow-and-green scheme that would give me subtle and satisfying contrasts and look good for five or six months.

YELLOWS AND GREENS

Stinking hellebore is very tough and Wester Flisk Group has purple-tinted leaf stalks and stems and blue-green leaves as well as the usual nodding clusters of green flowers. I set up two of these beneath a pair of yellow-stemmed dogwoods and variegated *Euonymus*.

The yellow theme continued to spill over the pot rim in the form of my favourite, yellow conifer – *Chamaecyparis pisifera* 'Filifera Aurea' – with its threads of thin foliage. Apple-green needled shore juniper also makes a fine drape alongside. All these plants are available in pots from garden retailers.

△ *Cracked pots can often be bought at a knock-down price. I repaired my giant pot with silicon sealant and then I rolled it under the overhang of this twiggy mock orange (Philadelphus).*

△ *Frost damage to roots can be even more damaging than to the aerial parts of your plants, so in cold, penetrating weather work in a thick mulch of hay across the surface of the pot. In really cold areas place bubble-wrap around the pot as well.*

▷ *Once you've finished planting your yellow-and-green pot, overlap clay roof tiles around the base for decoration and to prevent mud splashing the sides.*

▷ *An edging of upturned flower pots looks great poking up through the snow – and is a bit of fun, too.*

Practical information

Here are some additional facts and figures to supplement and expand on the tips found throughout this book.

SELECTING BY SIZE

Container gardeners have never had it so good when buying their spring and summer bedding, for an ever-increasing choice of plant sizes is available by post or from garden centres. These range from small trays of seedlings ready for pricking out to mature plants that will give an almost-instant effect. In between these two extremes are mini-seedlings, each grown in individual compartments in a cell tray, and larger, plug-format plants (see page 16). *Begonia* and busy lizzies are the top sellers, but more adventurous plant varieties are introduced each year. I've successfully grown collections of basil, unusual tomatoes and even herbaceous perennials such as pinks, *Penstemon* and *Campanula* from plugs.

Buying youngsters may initially seem more costly than seed raising your bedding but if seed is expensive (F_1 *Pelargonium* for example) or requires considerable warmth to germinate and grow early in the year (*Lobelia*) you often end up making a saving.

A similar trend towards an increasing size range is evident among hardy nursery stock on the sales beds. Japanese maples for example can be bought as two-year-old seedlings, three- or four-year-old grafted plants of named varieties, or up to ten-year-old monsters.

In *Non-stop Containers* I have at times introduced larger, specimen-sized shrubs and perennials, particularly in recipes where instant impact is required. Such mature heathers, hellebores, pinks, *Aubrieta*, gentians and *Hosta* are all well worth buying in order to create a balanced spread of foliage and flowers in your container display.

WEIGHTS

As well as heights, diameters and, where relevant, length and width, I have included the empty weights of each container to give you an idea of what you'll be lifting when you get your purchase home. Always lift with a straight back and knees bent. Heavy concrete and outsized terracotta pots are best moved on the base plate of a two-wheeled sack barrow. If you haven't got one, you may be able to borrow one from the garden centre. As the name implies, they are also the perfect vehicle to transport heavy sacks of potting compost too.

DRAINAGE

Good drainage is vital for a container-grown plant, especially in winter. Waterlogged roots will die through lack of oxygen. If your containers fill with water and freeze solid, they may burst. Many traditional gardeners rely on broken shards of terracotta (crocks) as drainage material. However broken chunks of polystyrene are increasingly popular, more readily available and less likely to add appreciably to the weight of the container. A good tip is to place a layer of horticultural fleece over the polystyrene chunks to act as a filter, thereby preventing compost and drainage material from mixing and possibly becoming clogged.

POTTING COMPOST

Most of the planting schemes in *Non-stop Containers* have been grown in Arthur Bowers peat-based, multi-purpose potting compost, from sowing right through to the final display pot. If you prefer to avoid a peat-based compost, use a mix based on coir (coconut fibre), or a mix of coir and a soil-based John Innes-type compost. Lime-hating plants such as *Rhododendron* must always be planted in an ericaceous (lime-free) compost. When planting, always use fresh potting compost in the container, and top up with fresh compost each time you replace a spent plant.

WATERING AND FEEDING

You can't rely on rainfall to water your containers. Even after a heavy shower the potting compost will still be dry below the moist surface crust. Establish a regular watering and feeding regime and you'll have prize-winning displays.

Give each pot a thorough soaking – enough to wet it through from top to bottom. A hose-end lance and nozzle are both convenient and labour saving. Aim to water before signs of wilting are evident, avoiding bright sunlight so plants don't scorch. To increase the moisture-retaining capacity of potting compost, you could mix in some water-retaining granules at the manufacturer's recommended rate, but don't use potting compost with water-retaining granules in winter.

Fertilisers replace nutrients used up by the plants and those leached out through watering, so feeding is essential to maintain plant health and vigour and to keep the flowers coming. A balanced one is best for mixed plantings. Solid or dry fertilisers can be mixed in with the compost, applied as a top dressing or pushed into the compost surface. Some last a whole season. Alternatively apply liquid feeds every 7–10 days. Start feeding 4–6 weeks after planting.

Index

In this index of suggested and actual plant ingredients in Non-stop Containers *the numbers in bold indicate photographs or their captions.*

Author's acknowledgements

Containers used in the following recipes were provided by the manufacturer or supplier named:

ANTIQUED CONCRETE URN
(pp.114–17)
Hampshire Garden Craft
BASKETWORK POT AND PANS
(pp.86–9)
Pembridge Terracotta
CHERUB TERRACOTTA POTS
(pp.24–9)
C.H. Brannam Ltd
DECORATED TERRACOTTA POTS
(pp.66–9)
C.H. Brannam Ltd
GIANT DECORATED POT
(pp.132–9)
Whichford Pottery
OVAL TERRACOTTA POT
(pp.16–19)
Whichford Pottery
SALT-GLAZED BOWL AND JARS
(pp.34–9)
Errington Reay Ltd
SIMULATED-STONE TROUGH
(pp.128–31)
Bradstone Pots & Planters
TERRACOTTA URN (pp.50–5)
C.H. Brannam Ltd
WOODEN TUBS (pp.60–5)
Trevis Smith Ltd

Contact addresses for details of stockists/availability

BRADSTONE POTS & PLANTERS,
Camas Building Materials,
Hulland Ward,
Ashbourne,
Derbyshire DE6 3ET
tel. 01335 372222

C.H. BRANNAM LTD,
Roundswell Industrial Estate,
Barnstaple,
Devon EX31 3NJ
tel. 01271 43035

ERRINGTON REAY LTD,
Tyneside Pottery Works,
Bardon Mill,
Hexham,
Northumberland NE47 7HU
tel. 01434 344245

HAMPSHIRE GARDEN CRAFT,
Rake Industries,
Rake,
Petersfield,
Hants GU31 5DR
tel. 01730 895182

PEMBRIDGE TERRACOTTA,
Pembridge,
Leominster,
Herefordshire HR6 9HB
tel. 01544 388696

TREVIS SMITH LTD,
Portersfield Road,
Cradley Heath,
West Midlands B64 7BZ
tel. 01384 569581

WHICHFORD POTTERY,
Whichford,
Shipston-on-Stour,
Warwickshire CV36 5PG
tel. 01608 684416

SOURCING OTHER CONTAINERS

- Oak half barrels can be bought from garden centres or petrol station forecourts
- New willow baskets can be found in florists' shops and garden centres; old ones in charity shops or car boot sales.
- Tin baths and, more rarely, watercarts turn up in salvage yards and auctions.
- Hay carts and potato harvesting baskets can be found at antique fairs and country shows.
- Imported glazed, mud and terracotta pots and bowls can be bought from garden centres, DIY superstores and garden shows. Home-made terracotta containers can be found at similar outlets or traced back to the potteries where they are made.
- Blue plastic containers are available from most DIY outlets.

SOURCING PLANTS

National garden shows are good places to track down and often buy from nurseries that specialise in rare and unusual plants. Alternatively you can visit the nursery itself or, if applicable, use its mail-order service.

Young plants can also be bought by mail order from many specialist firms as well as seed companies that include a young plant section in their catalogues. *The RHS Plant Finder* is an excellent, annual plant-hunters' guide to 70,000 plants and where to buy them.

Special thanks to the INTERNATIONAL FLOWER BULB CENTRE for supplying bulbs and to WEBBS GARDEN CENTRE, Wychbold, Droitwich, Worcestershire for help with seasonal and hardy plants from their extensive range.

All photographs were taken by myself using 35mm and medium-format cameras.

I would like to thank Shirley Patton, Helen Griffin, Joanna Chisholm and Bill Mason for their skills in bringing *Non-stop Containers* to fruition and Nicky Holden for posing for photographs.